ANGEL MAKERS:

HOW THE VICTORIAN'S ENCOURAGED BABY FARMING

Margaret Drinkall

Chris Drinkall

Contents

Introduction
Chapter One: Infanticide in Victorian Britain
Chapter Two: : Charlotte Winsor and Mary Jane Harris.
Chapter Three: Matilda Thorne and Caroline Jagger
Chapter Four: Annie Cummings
Chapter Five: Margaret Waters and Sarah Ellis.
Chapter Six: Susan King
Chapter Seven: Betsy Binmore
Chapter Eight: Sophia Martha Todd and Mary Dennis
Chapter Nine: John and Catherine Barnes
Chapter Ten: Annie Tooke
Chapter Eleven: Alice Reeves
Chapter Twelve: Mary Boyle
Chapter Thirteen: Ada Chard Williams
Chapter Fourteen: Conclusion

Introduction

This book is not a pleasant or easy book to research or read, but it will hopefully disturb the reader enough to question how circumstances allowed such a crime to flourish in an already brutal age. Many of the details of the death of these children will horrify us today, but sadly they are all true. It has to be said that the Victorian age was a time when, due to disease and poverty, many children would not survive after their fifth birthday. Nevertheless the very thought of the way in which these poor children died, revolted the Victorians of the period. What is generally accepted today is that literally hundreds, if not thousands, of children died at the hands of these baby farmers. The most disturbing aspect of it all however, was that legislation was powerless to prevent its spread. Critics of the system stated that the mothers of such children were equally to blame for the explosion of the increase of baby farming. They were accused of being accomplices in the crime, for which they deserved equal punishment with the women who killed or allowed their babies to die. One of the most prolific and infamous baby farmers was a woman called Amelia Dyer, who was hanged in 1896. Sadly there were many more of these women in Britain, whose crimes were not so well reported, and who are included in this book.

It is now an accepted fact, that the main element in the rise of the Victorian baby farmers was a piece of legislation, which was the Bastardy Clause of the Poor Law Act of 1834. This Act relieved men of all financial responsibility for their illegitimate children, placing the sole responsibility squarely on the woman's shoulders. Now pregnant mothers of illegitimate children had no recourse to law. If they kept the baby, they would have to find work, and if they wanted to work they must find someone to look after the baby. It was a simple fact that the majority of cases looking for a baby farmer were unmarried, single women who had found themselves pregnant. If they were lucky enough to find a situation which would allow them to keep their baby, they could not let their employer know that they had given birth to an illegitimate child. Women would be sacked if it came to light, and this secrecy aided the baby farmers and prevented their detection. Many of these were ruthless women, who out of ignorance or with an eye to economy, starved the child or fed it unsuitable food. Not for nothing were these people called 'Angel Makers'. What also helped to spread the horror of such crimes were the prevalence of newspaper reports which appeared at the time. The tax on newspapers had been cut to 1d in 1836, which made them accessible to the working classes. Now all the shocking details of baby farmers, their arrest and trial could be read about at the breakfast table.

The writing of any book is usually a team effort and my grateful thanks go, as always, to my son Chris, whose advice and expertise is invaluable. I would also like to thank Nicola Holland for allowing me to use her picture of an angel, which appears on the cover of this book. I would also like to acknowledge Rachel Colley for her support. But most of all this book is dedicated to the mothers and children of the nineteenth century who were forced, by the constraints of society, to hand their children right into the hands of these terrible monsters.

Chapter One: Infanticide in Victorian Britain

Long before the Victorians heard about the crime of baby farming, they were well aware of the crime of infanticide in the towns and cities of Britain, as the bodies of children were regularly found buried or left to die on the streets. As a writer I admit to a great fascination with the Victorian era, but I remain horrified at the sheer number of these cases, which were avidly reported in the local newspapers. Following the finding of these little bodies inquests were held, and although it was suspected that these were illegitimate children whose mothers had abandoned them, there was little proof. As we have seen women of that era, finding themselves pregnant had no recourse to financial help, and the only resolution was to go into the workhouses. Parliament had considered the problem when the numbers of abandoned babies began to grow, but it was thought that by giving such women parish out relief, it would actually encourage national immorality. Nineteenth century Victorian paternalism saw the mother's in such cases as being the weaker vessel, and truly believed that she was totally to blame for bringing illegitimate children into the world, due to her own licentious behaviour. It was widely thought that illegitimate children would inherit its mother 'weak morals' and even in the workhouse, such children would need to be kept away from women and other children who were otherwise deemed to be 'respectable'.

In some respects therefore it was easier, after giving birth, to abandon a child in the streets, and many women chose this course. Some left their children in baskets at the doors of the workhouse, or on the steps of what they hoped would be a philanthropic family, who would take the child as their own. Such a case was publicized in April 1819 when a boy child was found by a watchman on duty at York Place, London at the door of a gentleman's house. When he found the child, the householder ordered the night watchman to take it to the police house. Thankfully in this case the mother arrived to claim the child about half an hour later. It is tempting to think that she watched the whole affair, frightened of what would become of her abandoned baby. Another pitiable case, which indicates the difficulty of committing such an act, was that of a young child called Horace Stracy. The mother abandoned the month old male child on a doorstep in Chester Place, Hyde Park, in November 1867 leaving with it a letter. At a weekly meeting of the guardians of the Paddington workhouse on Wednesday December 11 1867, Mr Cormack the master of the workhouse read the heartbreaking letter out, which begged:

'Pray take pity on my poor little one. Don't think I am an unkind mother to thus cast him off, but I cannot see him want. There are homes and institutions supported by the benevolent where he can be well cared for, I know, but I have no power to get him in. You can, good friends do something for him, and God will reward you. But oh don't send him to the workhouse and dare I beg you a further favour? Would you, to ease the mind of an anxious and I may say a broken hearted mother, advertise in the "Daily Telegraph" of the 24 December just to let me know my little one is safe? Yes, to hear that will make it a happy Christmas for me indeed. Be sure it is hard for me to do this; but who would see her babe want?'

Others took on a more murderous way of ridding themselves of an unwanted child. On Sunday 18 November 1821 the body of a male child was found floating in the water in front of the Canal Hotel, Portobello. Marks of strangling were visible around the neck, and the verdict was that the child had been killed before being thrown in the water. What was particularly tragic about the discovery of this child was that it was judged to being between 6 and 8 months of age and described as a 'fine, well-looking boy having on him a cap and a good flannel petticoat'. This case reveal the tragedy of a woman who gave birth, and probably tried desperately to care for her child for several months, before eventually being driven to commit murder. The newspaper requested that 'if anyone knew of a mother who could not account for the disappearance of her child, to communicate with the local magistrates'. But the probability was that the identity of the mother was never discovered.

As the problems of infanticide was on the increase, the government brought in a piece of legislation to try to prevent deaths of children in 1836, when the law ordered that all births had to be registered. But this was only effective for legitimate children, and therefore the thousands of illegitimate births escaped the net. Such children remained unregistered, and hence unknown to the authorities. When the cases of infanticide were increasing to a degree which could not be ignored, the matter was discussed in the House of Commons in July 1863. This was announced following a statement on 'the appalling increase in infanticide in England' from the MP for Finsbury, Mr William Cox. He told the house that 'out of 5,547 inquests held in the capital the previous year, that 1,887 were held on the bodies of dead infants and of these the alarming figure of 224 had resulted in verdicts of willful murder'. He urged the Government to take the question into their serious consideration and asked the Home Secretary, Sir George Grey for a reply during the recess. But the only solution that Sir George could offer was completely unworkable. He replied that 'the best means of checking the crime of infanticide was to improve the morals of the people, for which no law that Parliament could frame, would be so effectual to prevent it'. By 1863, what people didn't realise, was that the problems of infanticide was being exacerbated by the baby farmers, and it could not be solely blamed on girls disposing themselves of their illegitimate children. Only when the full scale horror of the business was uncovered, did the Victorians accept that this vile trade had been escalating and was responsible for many of the abandoned babies.

Finding a person to look after a child was easy enough, as most of these cases advertised to 'nurse' or 'adopt' a child in local newspapers. There were women who would look after a child for a few shillings a week, whilst others would 'adopt' a child for a one-off fee. The reality proved that many of these children were eliminated when they had served their usefulness, when the mother had stopped paying the few pence a week for childcare, or a short while after the child had been 'adopted'. Under the cover of darkness such children were merely abandoned in the streets, alive or dead. Others had a more lingering death at the hands of these monsters by starving them slowly, or feeding them inappropriately. The conditions of the houses of the baby farmers were usually unsanitary and disgusting, and there is little evidence of the children who died from diseases caught under such an environment.

The baby farmers were not ignorant women and many of them were crafty and manipulative. These vicious women appealed directly to mothers, desperate to give their child a better life than they were able to. One such advertisement purporting to come from a respectable widow was inserted in the *Morning Post* of September 1867 requesting:

'WANTED the CARE of a LADY'S CHILD' by a widow of the highest respectability who has lost several of her own and in whom the greatest confidence can be placed'. Apply MPT, Post Office Ealing Broadway'.

In all these cases the name of the 'widow' concerned were always anonymous, and the collection point to pick up the replies was usually a busy local Post Office. The child was usually handed over at a crowded railway station, which encouraged anonymity. Once the vile trade of baby farming was brought to prominence, newspaper proprietors were condemned for carrying such adverts. The *Pall Mall Gazette* of Wednesday 25 September 1867 asked:

'How this monstrous system can be arrested is a question demanding earnest consideration? One thing, at any rate, can admit of no dispute - that a heavy responsibility rests on those journals which lends themselves to the promotion of such a trade'.

Once a financial agreement was made, the child was swiftly handed over to the nurse or adoptive mother who would usually be paid in cash or postage stamps. Some women made arrangements to see their baby on a regular basis where possible, but always she had to bear in mind that if her employers found out, it would result in instant dismissal. This concealment protected the baby farmers as they continued to flourish under the umbrella of secrecy.

Other desperate mothers were prepared to let their little child be adopted in the hope that their secret would never be found out. This was a gift to the baby farmers, who always made an agreement stating that the mother would make no claim on them in the future, almost certainly securing the child's demise. One advertisement in the *Bristol Mercury* of August 15 1863 requested:

'WANTED to ADOPT a BABY from its birth, by married persons without children - Address Baxter, Post Office, Bath'.

Ominously the following month the same advert requested 'small premium required'. Underneath was another 'wanted child to adopt' advert, which stated categorically the cost would be a one-off payment of £30. By July 29 of the same year, the same newspaper columns were carrying adverts almost every week from 'respectable couple with no children of their own' wishing to adopt or nurse a child. The *Daily News* called attention to the danger of this kind of trade. It stated:

'there are always parties quite as anxious to get rid of a child, as these good people can be to have the delight of infant company. Children are daily born for whom human forethought has provided no place. What a relief to the distressed parents or of the distressed parent's friends to know, that it is possible by the aid of a money payment to make one final provision for the little one, with the certainty of hearing no more of it. And yet society might reasonably doubt the sufficiency of the guarantees of the child's safety'.

Another fruitful way for baby farmers to obtain children were at 'lying-in houses' which were sometimes known as 'accouchement houses'. These were run by women who catered for pregnant women wishing to give birth in secret. They opened their own homes, where they were able to charge the mother for her stay, as well as making arrangements for the adoption of the child. These services were usually offered to better off women who were able to pay the required sums. Discreet adverts would be inserted into newspapers which stated:

'A WIDOW has FURNISHED APARTMENTS TO LET, for a person during confinement, or would take charge of one or two children - Address, Mrs RO'

Another such advertisement read:

'APARTMENTS for a Lady, strictly private, ready for immediate occupation. Every comfort and careful nursing, on very moderate terms. Baby linen provided - By letter, EP.'

A criticism of these houses was made in February 1868, not because of the services they offered, but because their very existence would lead to widespread general immorality. One particular newspaper was condemned once again for the insertion of such adverts within its pages, which offered in code, what might not be expressed in the advertisement. The *Daily Telegraph* regularly had at least half a dozen of these 'coded adverts blatantly within its columns'. Such houses described themselves as 'retirement homes for Ladies of delicate health' usually meant those women who were unmarried and pregnant. Some were less delicate and added the words 'the baby can be left'. Others promise a 'resident midwife, a highly trained, kind nurse and a physician found' to reassure that mother that medical help was also on offer. Aimed at higher class women who were able to afford such luxuries, these adverts would include a 'drawing room with a piano' and more prosaically that 'gas and all requisites were provided'. By March 1868 the *Telegraph* was pressurized to cease all such adverts for this sort of trade.

The *British Medical Journal* took it upon itself to take a closer look at some of these better off establishments. An unnamed doctor answered such an advert for these homes and his report was published in the *BMJ* in June 1865. On the appointed day he had arrived at the lying-in house, whose door was opened by a young woman aged about 33 years of age. The physician reported that the house was neat and in a quiet street, and he was shown into what the doctor described as a prettily furnished parlour. The fire was burning and opposite it was a good looking piano, and the whole house gave off a 'well to do aspect'. He asked owner of the house 'did she take women to be confined' and she stated that she did 'either for long or short periods, at terms which included doctors fees'. She pointed out that she always used her own doctor, and that a separate sitting room was available for the mother if required. She explained that if the lady was almost ready to give birth, the baby could be adopted and sent into the country on payment of a sum of money. If, however the woman was not far gone in her pregnancy, then her stay would be longer and the sum would obviously be higher. The doctor asked her 'was there any danger for the mother or child' and she replied 'no dear, it is perfectly safe' pointing out that she had been in the business for 12 years and had never had any 'mishaps'. She told him that he could speak to her own doctor for a reference, 'who had attended thousands of cases at her house where women had been confined'.

At another house that advertised such services, the same doctor was invited in by a man aged about 55 years, who stated that he was the husband of the woman he had come to see. He showed the physician into the parlour where he was joined later by his wife, who was described as 'a sleek, plump woman'. She told him that she did take in ladies to be confined, but admitted that 'her costs of 50 guineas did not include wines, spirits beers, nor castor oil, nor did it include coals or medicine'. She would also require another 20 guineas for her own services, all of which had to be paid in advance, before admitting that she also dealt in the adoptions for these babies. Then she went into a more sinister part of the services which she offered, which was for women requiring an abortion. She told the doctor that:

'the lady could be attended to by wearing a veil over her face, and all she would be required to do was to lay on her side. She would then be given something; but she need not stop longer than a quarter of an hour, after which she must take a long walk'

The woman told the doctor that she never performed such an operation without a medical man being in attendance and had been in the business for 27 years. Chillingly she boasted that she was never short of patients, and that some others had come back six or seven times. The *BMJ* was praised for the underground work by exposing the fact that in many parts of London this 'trade' is carried on under the most flimsy disguise. Sometimes these women quite openly carried out 'a criminal trade equally dangerous to the morality and the health of the community, and constituting a felonious offence'. The *BMJ* stated that this trade 'affects all ranks of society' and they called upon the officers of the Metropolitan Police to stop such crimes.

The *Manchester Times* also ran an article which illustrated how lying-houses operated in December 1869. The report stated that what usually happens is that a 'lady' departs for the country in delicate health, and she returned from the country still delicate, but improving. At one of these house she leaves the 'consequences of her illness', who is left to be disposed of, on condition that it is never to be heard of again by its mother. A correspondent of a London newspaper wrote to *Cheshire Observer* asking for the editor to do a good service to investigate the advertisements offering 'Quiet apartments for a Lady'. The correspondent writes:

'I know one house where 14 children were born in one month, all taken away the morning after birth, and some of the ladies away home again in a fortnight. It is most usual to give

birth to a "seven month" child and then pay £50 to be relieved of all further trouble and expense. After giving birth the nurse takes charge of the infant and farms it out. Scarcely ever is a register of birth made; in fact these places are little less than murder dens, and should indeed be most carefully inspected and licensed'.

The exploits of one of these houses were uncovered whilst a case of fraud was being investigated in December 1870 by a woman called Mary Hall. She had kept a 'lying in' establishment at Cold Harbour Lane, South London, where evidence was found from books on the premises that at least 46 ladies had been confined there. Superintendent Gernon of the Metropolitan Police Force established that some women had paid from £10 to £15 a week for board and lodgings whilst they were being confined. When they were interviewed, none of them knew what had happened to their children, except that Mrs Hall had arranged to have them adopted. It certainly seems to have been a lucrative business, as property to the value of £800 had been found in Mrs Hall house, as well as a number of IOU's which had been given to her by ladies confined there. Once again the blame for these children's deaths were placed on the mothers who left their child with such unscrupulous women. Coroners who held the many inquests into the deaths of these children, begged that mothers be warned against leaving them in the hands of such plausible strangers. Letters from Mrs Hall to some of the mothers were read out in the inquiry, which were reported to be 'couched in the most artful and endearing terms'.

As police investigations started to be made on the houses and the women who ran them, the officers found their task was most difficult. At that time there was many ways for these monsters to evade capture, and the most prevalent was to simply disappear. Victorian Britain had no efficient police force at that time, and they had few ways of accurately checking identities. Baby farmers who were being investigated would simply change their names and addresses, and set up business in a different area. But it was the case of Amelia Dyer which brought the wholesale murders committed by baby farming to the newspaper reading public and to the world. The case of Dyer has been the subject of many books, and people were appalled when the case came to the public attention in 1896 when she was finally caught and hung. Now called the most prolific serial killer, it was thought that throughout her career, which lasted over twenty years, she killed as many as 400 children. What was also revealed by police investigations was that the women who carried out these terrible crimes came from very diverse backgrounds. Many were poor ignorant, working class women, intent on deriving some employment by a method which took the least energy. Others were middle class women (one was a former governess) who were very clever and manipulative. But whatever background they came from, they all spun the same story; offering a place to bring up a child in much better circumstances than could be provided by a poor, ignorant, single mother. These are some of their stories. Many of these monsters got away with a prison sentence, whilst others received the ultimate punishment on the gallows for their crimes.

Chapter Two: Charlotte Winsor and Mary Jane Harris.

The first case of baby farming which came to light was reported in 1865, when the trial of Charlotte Winsor and Mary Jane Harris exposed to the public the horrific trade in children. People were, quite naturally, appalled at the exploits of such women, one of whom was prepared to murder children without mercy for small sums of money. Although it was unknown at this time Amelia Dyer had already started her murderous career in 1846, but it was this case that brought baby farming to public attention. What also makes this case very unusual, was the fact that one of the murders was done with the complicity of the mother.

On 15 February 1865, Mr Thomas Millman was walking along a fairly isolated road at Cockington, near Torquay, and he was accompanied by another man called Edwin Selby. The two men spotted a parcel lying on a piece of rough ground, about two feet from a hedge. There was snow on the ground and the parcel, which was made up of some blue worsted material, was sewn together with blue stitching. Selby took out his penknife and cut two or three of the stitches, before looking inside to see what the parcel contained. Millman noticed some newspaper, which he pulled to one side and both men were horrified to find the body of a child. They immediately took the body to the Torquay police station, where it was quickly handed it over to Police Constable William Ford. The police surgeon was called, and he told them that the body was that of a five or six month old male baby. The wrapping found around the child was a newspaper, which was the *Western Times* dated May 6 1864.

The police made enquiries and they soon heard of a servant girl who had recently given birth, and they found that most unusually the child's birth had been registered. His name was given as Thomas Edwin Gibson Harris, and that his mother was a servant girl named Mary Jane Harris aged 23, who had given birth four months previously. The father of the child was said to be a local farmer called Nicholls, a man of some substance in the area, who had previously had another illegitimate child, a little girl who was in the care of a woman in Torquay. On 20 February Sergeant John Edwards went to the house of the nurse who was caring for the child in Torquay and found she was called Mrs Harriet Gibson of Higher Union Lane. She admitted that Mary Jane Harris had been at her house when she gave birth to a male child on 16 October 1864. The mother and child, who she called Tommy, had stayed with her until 12 November when Harris had gained a position as a cook and had gone into service. Sergeant Edwards asked Mrs Gibson if she knew where Harris was now, and she gave him the address of the girl's employer. The next day the sergeant went to speak to the girl at the house of Mrs Wansey of Tamar Villas, Warren Road, Torquay. He asked Mrs Wansey if he might interview her cook privately and the girl was brought into the parlour by her mistress. After some hesitation and nervous glances towards her employer, Harris finally admitted that she had given birth to a child in October. It was the first time that her employer had known that Harris had a baby, and she didn't look too pleased about the news.

The girl told Sergeant Edwards that when she gave birth to the baby, that Mrs Gibson had told her that she knew a woman who offered to nurse or adopt babies. The woman's name was Charlotte Winsor. Harris had met Winsor who was aged about 45 and she left the child with her, and agreed to pay her 3s 6d a week for Tommy's keep. On 23 February Sergeant Edwards went to speak to Winsor, who lived in an isolated farmhouse situated on the Newton Road, just outside Torquay. He found her at home with her husband, and a grand daughter, a girl of eight called Selina Pratt. The sergeant asked Winsor if she was looking after Harris's child, and if the baby was still there. She told him that the child's mother, and a woman who she said was Harris's aunt, had taken Tommy away about three weeks previously. She described the aunt as being 'a tallish woman, with a dark complexion, wearing a dark bonnet, coloured shawl, an alpaca gown and was aged about forty years of age'. She also described the child as being 'a plumpish child, with a long thin nose, rather light complexion, between dark and light hair'. She added 'I hope that nothing has happened to the pretty dear'. Sergeant Edwards was immediately aware that the description given by Winsor, did not fit that of the remains of the child that had been found. He asked to speak to the grand daughter Selina, and asked her if she could remember the last day that she had seen little Tommy. The girl told him that at some time around the beginning of February, she had been asked by her grandmother to go on an errand. Selina left the house and said that little Tommy was sitting on her grandmother's knee when she went out. The sergeant asked her if Harris was also there, and she told him that she was. When the girl returned, the baby had gone and when she asked her grandmother where Tommy was, Selina was told that Harris's aunt had taken the child away. Harris, who was still there, confirmed the story. She told the girl that she had met her aunt at the station and had given her the baby to care for. Selina told Sergeant Edwards that her grandmother had then given her two pence and asked her to go out again and buy two buns for their tea. It took her about half an hour to get the buns, and she never saw little Tommy again.

The police decided that it was now time to re-interview the child's mother, and Police Sergeant Edwards was sent once again, to the house where Harris was employed. He asked her if her aunt was also called Harris, but she told him that had been her maiden name, but she had since married and was called Stephens now. Mrs Stephens was then traced to Exeter and questioned, but she told the police that she hadn't seen Harris for over a year. When she was informed of what her aunt had said, the girl broke down crying. After a moment or two she asked Sergeant Edwards 'the child that was found, it is mine isn't it?' The officer admitted that the child had been identified as hers by Mrs Gibson. He also told her that he was not happy with her story, and took her to the police station where she was arrested. As they were walking to the station Harris said 'if I cannot give a true account of what happened to my child, will I be hung?' He told her that she would have to be tried at the assizes first, and she was crying as he put her into a cell at the police station. After a very short time of being in custody, she admitted to PC Thomas Verco that 'Mrs Winsor has done it' and to the horrified constable told him 'she has put away many children'. The constable took her to a room in the station, where accompanied by Sergeant Edwards, the girl made a terrible confession. As the constable wrote down her statement, Harris described how Charlotte Winsor had told her that she had murdered one child who was three weeks old, when she threw it into the bay at Torquay; and another she had carried out to the moors and left it to die.

The following day Harris was interviewed again by Sergeant Edwards, and she described how she had met Mrs Winsor and how she had made arrangements for her to care for little Tommy. Unbeknownst to Harris, on the same day as she was making her statement, Charlotte Winsor, herself went to the police station and asked about what was happening to the girl. She told the desk sergeant that 'they tell me that she is here for murdering her child. I don't believe she has' and once again repeated the lie that the child had been taken away by her aunt. She was shown the body of the recovered child and she flatly denied that it was Harris's, as she told the police that 'Tommy had a wart on his toes'. Selina Pratt was also interviewed again, and she stated that a day or so after she had been told that Tommy had been taken away by his aunt, she saw her grandmother ironing some of the baby's clothes. Later that same night, she went out with her grandmother and said 'at a certain place my grandmother told me to stay where I was, whilst she went up a hill'. The constable interviewing her asked her if she could remember the exact spot, and she told him that she could. The child was taken to the area and she pointed out the place where her grandmother had told her to wait. It was near to the same place where the dead child's body had been found.

The police returned back to the house of Charlotte Winsor and searched the property. There they found a pile of newspapers which proved to be the *Western Times,* which was the same newspaper that had been wrapped around the body of the child. They closely examined the dates of each one, and found that only the edition that was wrapped around the child was missing. Although they searched the house from top to bottom they could not find the newspaper dated May 6 1864. An inquest was held on the child's remains on Friday 18 February 1865, where the Coroner announced that he would not keep the jury long as he was just intending to deal with the identification of the child that day. He said that he would then adjourn the inquest in order for the police to continue with their enquiries. Mrs Harriet Gibson gave evidence that she had taken Mary Jane Harris into her house where she had been confined of a child on 16 October, and where she remained for the next few weeks. She confirmed that the child was a boy and she told the Coroner that he was fine healthy child, very fair with round features and auburn hair. Mrs Gibson was asked by the Coroner if the child had a wart on its foot, and she denied it strongly. The witness told the jury that she had gone with Harris to see Mrs Charlotte Winsor who agreed to take the child. On the previous Thursday she had gone to the Torquay Town Hall to look at the body of the child that had been found. Mrs Gibson stated that she had identified it as the child that had been born to Mary Jane Harris. The inquest was then adjourned for a week

When the inquest was reconvened on Monday 27 February the police surgeon, Mr William W Stabb had undertaken the post mortem on the body. He stated that before the baby died he had eaten a meal, and he deduced that the child had probably died within the next half an hour. He said that externally there were no marks on the body, and it appeared to be a well nourished, healthy infant. After examining the organs, which were all healthy, he came to the opinion that the child had died of suffocation, and there were no signs of external violence. Harris told the inquest that after Mrs Winsor had the child for three weeks, she had arrived at her employer's house demanding money, that she said she was owed which amounted to 1s 6d. Harris who was frantic that her employer would not find out about little Tommy told her that she hadn't any money, and Mrs Windsor told her to ask her employer for advancement on her wages. Harris asked Mrs Wansey for the money without giving the reason why, and her employer gave her 1s 6d which she then gave to Winsor. Mrs Harriet Gibson then gave the most damning evidence on the complicity of Mary Jane Harris in the murder of 'little Tommy'. She told the Coroner that she had met Harris on 2 May, four days before the child was killed, and when she asked how 'little Tommy was doing', she was told that she was intending taking the child away from Mrs Winsor's and placing it with her aunt. The girl stated that her aunt had no children of her own, and she had agreed to look after little Tommy for 2s a week, which was a complete fabrication. The Coroner questioned her on her evidence, which only emphasized that Harris was well aware in advance of what Winsor planned to do with the baby. After hearing all the evidence, the jury retired for only a short while, before returning a verdict of wilful murder against both Mary Jane Harris and Charlotte Winsor. Winsor left the room looking very thoughtful, but Harris was sobbing as she was led away. The two women appeared at the magistrates court on Wednesday 29 February where Sergeant John Edwards gave evidence that when Charlotte Windsor's house had been searched, he had noted that there was a ball of blue worsted wool, which was the same wool used to wrap up the parcel containing the dead child.

Harris's employer, Mrs Wansey gave evidence that in November, Harris had gone to work for her as a cook and that she paid her £12 a year. She told the magistrates that she had a high opinion of her employee, and that she worked hard and was a 'well conducted and kindly girl'. Mrs Betsy Stephens gave evidence that the prisoner Harris was her niece and that she had two other aunts, Sarah Ann Barker and Eliza Harris. She told the magistrates that she did not even know that her niece had a child, until the police went to her house to enquire if she had the baby. She categorically told the magistrate that she did not go to Mrs Winsor's house, nor meet her niece at the station in order to pick up a child. When she had seen her niece at the police station she asked her 'why did you say I had the child' and Harris replied 'I did not know what to say'. Then the magistrate summed up the case for the jury, who took just twenty minutes to find both women guilty of the murder of four month old Tommy Harris and the two women were ordered to take their trial at the next assizes. The trial of Mary Jane Harris and Charlotte Winsor took place at the Devon Lent Assizes on Friday 17 March 1865 before Judge Baron Channell. Mr Carter and Mr Montague Bere were counsel for the prosecution and Mr Prideaux and Mr Turner were the defence counsel for Harris and Mr Folkard for Winsor.

The first witness was Sergeant John Edwards who described finding the bundle of *Western Times* newspapers, out of which the edition for May 6 had been missing. PC William Ford gave evidence about Thomas Millman handing in the body of the child to him on 15 February. He described how he had unwrapped the bundle and found the newspaper covering the whole body of the child, whose hands were folded across its chest and his legs were drawn up in a sitting position. PC Ford also told the judge about a meeting between Harris and Winsor after they had both been arrested. He was escorting Harris into a room in the Town Hall for another interview, when the two women saw each other. When Winsor saw Harris she said to her 'how do you do Mary' and then drew a finger across her throat, whilst looking directly at her. PC Robert Evans told the court that he went to Winsor's cell after she had been arrested on 25 February; she told him that she knew that Mary Jane Harris was guilty and she 'hoped that she would be transported'. He stated that when Winsor was taken into custody, she claimed that Harris had killed the child and added that 'it wasn't the first time that she had tried to kill little Tommy'. She related an incident which she said had occurred one night when Harris had been at her house for most of the day. Harris had the child on her lap and Winsor claimed that she saw her give the baby something that looked like sugary candy. After a moment Winsor picked up the child and put her tongue to its mouth, when Harris said to her 'don't taste it, it'll poison you'. When Winsor asked what it was that she had given the child, Harris told her that it was something 'they gave to kill rats and mice'. The constable related how Winsor had told him that Harris had said that she had got it from her employer, and that she had been using it for cleaning brass and copper. Winsor then told him that she had got some milk and water for the child to drink, to get rid of the poison given to it by its mother.

Continuing with this incredible tale, she then said that she had gone outside and when she came back inside, Harris had put the child head first into some water. Winsor had pulled the child out of the water, telling her 'do you mean to hang yourself and me too'. At this point in the trial it was agreed that it would be adjourned until the following day, and arrangements were made for the jury to be accommodated for the night at the White Horse Inn. The judge warned them that they must not speak to anyone about the trial, and they were supervised by one of the court officials. The following day the first witness was Selina Pratt. The girl exhibited no signs of nervousness as she told the court that when little Tommy came to her grandmother's house, the baby had plenty of clothes with it. The girl described the boys clothing, which we would now consider to be girl's clothes, but which were traditional for that period. They consisted of three frocks, three aprons, two chemises, three bands and two flannel petticoats. Selina said that the little boy had stayed at her grandmother's house for a month, until the night he disappeared. She described how she was told by Harris that he had gone to her aunt's house. One of the jurors asked her whether Harris had told her this in front of her grandmother, and she told him that she had. Selina then described the journey with her grandmother and the carpet bag. She told the court that on her return the bag was empty. The judge asked her 'how did you know it was empty' and she told him that she knew it was because she was carrying it. To a startled court she stated that she also said that they had been out on other occasions with the same carpet bag. The medical evidence from Mr Stabb showed that the baby had died from asphyxiation.

Then it was Mr Folkard turn to present the case for the Winsor's defence. He remarked on her 'affectionate character' and he emphasized the improbability that she could commit such an barbarous act. He also brought a character witness, a woman called Mary Barber, who had known Winsor for many years. She said that the prisoner was particularly 'kind and attentive in cases of illness and sorrow, and that she had always found her to be honest and truthful woman'. Mr Prideaux, Harris's defence counsel, also claimed that his client could not have been guilty of such an act on her own child 'which had not been proved to his satisfaction'. He produced a copy of the register of the child's birth certificate and he asked the jury 'if they really felt sure that the dead child was that of the prisoner's, why would she go to the bother of registering the child if she truly intended to do away with it?' He reminded them that much of the evidence had been given by an eight year old child, who might easily have been mistaken. The defence counsel warned the jury that if Selina had been mistaken, then the dead child might have been a complete stranger, but they still had to decide how that child had died. Mr Prideaux stated that a person 'cannot be convicted with having a passive knowledge of a murder, but the jury must be convinced that Mary Jane Harris had taken an active part in it'. The judge summed up for three hours, but the defence had cast so much doubt on the evidence, that even when the jury deliberated for another five hours, they could not agree on a verdict. Baron Channell had no option but to order that the case was to be re-heard at the next assizes.

On Friday July 28 1865 the two women were placed in the dock of the Exeter Assizes, before Mr Justice Keating. To the surprise of the court, and possibly to prevent another 'hung jury', the counsel for the prosecution started by requesting his lordship to allow Mary Jane Harris to be a witness against Charlotte Winsor. He asked that it be allowed as 'his learned friend and himself were of the opinion that the ends of justice required it'. Winsor looked at the prisoner Harris with venom, as she was then removed from the dock. Harris watched her former friend with dispassion as she was taken out of the court. She then stood up in the dock and made the following terrible confession. She stated that she had been walking through the town of Torquay with Charlotte Winsor when she told her that 'a child had been found and there was going to be trouble ahead for them both'. Winsor had admitted that 'I wonder how I had not got myself into it before' and then confessed to a number of murders of other children she had nursed. She told her of one case where a girl had been confined at her house, and had promised her £3 to have the child adopted. Winsor had agreed but when the girl had recovered she went away to get the money, leaving the child. When the girl did not return with the money as promised, Winsor admitted that she had killed it. Harris asked her how she did it, and Winsor told her that she simply put her finger under the jugular vein. The prisoner told the, now deathly quiet court, that Winsor had also confessed to having killed another child belonging to woman called Elizabeth Darwin. Harris described how Winsor had told her that she threw the baby into the water at Torquay and cackled as she callously admitted that 'when it was found, it had been in the water for so long that it had dropped to pieces'. Winsor admitted that she had also disposed of a baby for her sister, who gave her £4 to have it adopted, although she had only paid her £2. After this confession Harris, had asked Winsor if 'she was afraid' but the callous woman simply told her that she was 'doing good'.

Harris told the jury, that she had been at Winsor's house in February when the woman offered to get rid of little Tommy and she had refused. However a month later Winsor offered again to dispose of Tommy for £5. Harris told her that she did not have £5 to give her. Winsor told her to get the money from the father of the child, who was known to be well off, but Harris told her she could not do that either. Winsor boasted that 'if she had forty children she could easily get rid of them for her'. Harris's voice faltered, as she described how a short while later, she had finally agreed to let Winsor 'get rid' of Tommy. Harris had asked Winsor how she would do it and she replied that she would 'get something from the chemist'. On Sunday 5 May Harris went to Winsor's house and watched as her baby sat in a chair and Selina played with him. After the two women had sat talking a little while, Winsor sent out her grand daughter on an errand. She told Harris that 'she would do it while she was there, which would make them both guilty, and therefore Harris would not be able to tell on her'. The girl asked Winsor how she would do it and the woman said that she would put the baby between two bed ticks (mattresses). Winsor then went into Selina's bedroom with the baby. Harris described to a horrified court that Winsor was only in the bedroom about ten minutes before came out without the baby, who had not made a sound. When Selina returned, she was told that baby Tommy had gone to Harris's aunt before Winsor sent her out to fetch some buns.

When her granddaughter had gone out again, the baby farmer told Harris that 'we must make haste' and went back into the bedroom where she quickly emerged with the body of the dead child. The two women went into Winsor's bedroom where she found a box with some clothes in it. Harris took out the clothes and they placed the body of the baby inside and Winsor locked it and put the key in her pocket. Winsor told Harris that she would dispose of it later. Harris then told the court that she went back to work at her mistress's house and continued with her duties. She told the judge that after she had been apprehended, she had asked Winsor if the child that had been found was little Tommy, and the woman admitted that she thought it was. Harris described seeing Winsor again in gaol and asking her once more if she had carried the baby up onto the moor, and Winsor immediately admitted that she had. At this point Harris was cross examined by the prosecution, who asked her to clarify that she had willingly left her baby 'with this woman, who had confessed to killing other children'. As Harris admitted that she had, she was asked bluntly 'if at this point she had wanted the child to die'. Harris said that she didn't want it to die, but told the court that the father of the child, a man she referred to as Farmer Nicholls had promised to pay for him to be at Winsor's, but he had paid her nothing. Harris told the court that she had allowed her child to die because Charlotte had 'filled her mind up with it, and she was led away by her'. The prisoner concluded her statement by saying that 'her conscience had induced her to speak the truth, and she did not expect to be pardoned'. The witness was incredibly calm whilst she gave her evidence, but the officials of the court and the witnesses were visibly shocked at her confession.

At that point the prosecution, Mr Carter stated that he should have to bring Charlotte Winsor back into the court, and when she heard that, Harris cried bitterly. She visibly flinched as Winsor was placed beside her in the dock. As her statement was read out, Winsor too appeared shocked, hearing that she was condemned out of Harris' mouth. The defence for Winsor, Mr Folkard pointed out that disturbing as the statement made by Harris was, that her evidence could not be taken as truth, as it was entirely uncorroborated by any other witness. He also pointed out that it was in Winsor's own interest to keep the child alive as she was being paid 3s 6d a week for it. The judge confirmed for the jury that they did not have any obligation to believe in the evidence of an accomplice, except when that the material was corroborated by other witnesses. He said that the prisoner Mary Jane Harris was an accomplice in this crime and there could be no doubt about that. He admitted that 'seldom had ears heard more hideous revelations than those made in the witness box by Harris'. The judge's summing up lasted for over two hours before the jury returned a verdict of guilty against Charlotte Winsor. The sentence of death was passed on her and throughout the judge's words Winsor cried convulsively. Harris was merely told that she was to remain in custody for the time being until a decision as made as to her own fate.

Charlotte Winsor was informed whilst in the condemned cell that she was to be executed on Friday 18 August 1865. Soon after this announcement Harris was pardoned and released. By 12 August there were grave doubts cast upon the legality of the first jury being discharged without a verdict, at the first assizes. The legal experts thought that Winsor had, in effect, been tried twice for the same crime which, as they pointed out, was contradictory to English Law. It was also noted that a jury cannot be discharged without the prisoners consent, or in the rare case where a member of a jury had died whilst on duty. The concerns were passed onto the Lord Chancellor, who considered that the subject should be put before a panel of judges for their decision. In order that this could be done, the execution of Charlotte Winsor, now described as 'a professional child murderer', was put off until Monday 27 November, in order that the whole matter could be thoroughly investigated. This decision caused disgust with a large number of people who had flocked to Exeter, eager to witness the hanging of this reviled baby farmer. It was stated in local newspapers that 'they could hardly be convinced that the hanging would not take place'. It was also reported that Calcraft the hangman had arrived in Exeter on the Thursday morning, and after being told of the respite, returned home the same night. On Monday November 20 the case of Charlotte Winsor was heard in the Court of the Queens Bench. Charlotte Winsor was brought before the court to give her evidence on Friday November 24, but the case was put off again until the following term. The following year on Tuesday 24 January 1866 the case was discussed once more, but the complicated points of law were very difficult to follow, even for experts. They took three days before a decision was made that the verdict of the crown was to be upheld, and the execution of Charlotte Winsor was therefore due to take place. Nevertheless on February 14 it was announced that the case was once again to be argued in the Exchequer Chamber, due to the fact that Mary Jane Harris had given evidence against Charlotte Winsor, without having been 'discharged from the indictment'. When Winsor was brought up to London to be presented at the Chambers for the case to be discussed, it was noted that where she used to be a stout woman, now the prisoner looked thin and careworn. During the long discussion by her counsel, Winsor never showed any emotion, but sat beneath the judge's bench with her eyes cast on the ground. At the end of two days of argument, it was agreed that no error had been made and finally agreed that the sentence was to be carried out.

The newspapers announced the following day that Winsor had written out a confession of all her crimes and had given it to friends who had visited on the previous Saturday. However the governor of Exeter gaol would not allow this to happen, and in retaliation the prisoner told him that 'she would write out another one and throw to people from the gallows'. When Winsor was visited by the chaplain and the prison governor to be told that another decision had been made and it was now agreed that she was to be respited for another month, she made no comment apart from saying 'its no odds what they do to me'.

Winsor was once more respited until 5 May, but also warned that she should hold out no hope that she would be released. Despite this, however it was announced on Friday 11 May 1866, almost a year after she had been found guilty, that Charlotte Winsor's sentence was to be commuted to one of life imprisonment. The papers were in uproar at the news that Winsor was not to be hanged. The fury at the woman and her crime forced the *Exeter Mercury* to announce that

'we can understand the recoil of horror at the idea of hanging a woman, but if feelings like these are to interfere with the administration of the law, then the sooner the law of capital punishment was abolished the better'.

Others like the *Sunday Gazette* applauded the decision giving as their reason that 'the mere legality of the conviction was far too questionable to allow it to be pushed to its logical and extreme conclusion'. It was strongly felt however that Charlotte Winsor had escaped her execution simply because Mary Jane Harris had lied to save herself. Harris knew that if she gave evidence against Charlotte Winsor, that she would be in a good position to be pardoned for her actions in the death of her son. Thankfully for the rest of her natural life Winsor was kept in prison, and it seemed to the newspaper reading public that at least one baby farmer had been kept off the streets. Almost thirty years later in April 1894 it was reported that Charlotte Winsor was 'now in Woking Female Convict Prison where she was about to complete her 30th year in prison'. It was reported that she was now 'an old woman whose confinement didn't seem to trouble her much'. But if the public were relieved that one baby farmer had been caught, what they did not realise was that many more were about to take her place.

Chapter Three: Matilda Thorne and Caroline Jagger

Two years later in the year of 1867 there were more cases which brought to the attention of the authorities the abysmal traffic in young children. The first case gives an indication into the low paid employment that women with illegitimate children were forced to undertake, to pay for their child care. It also illustrates the casual attitude that baby farmers had towards the children in their care. The horror which resonated with the reading public was that of a baby farmer who was quite clear about her role. In her own words she claimed that 'she was never short of babies and when one died, she simply advertised for another'. The second case is indicative of the shame which giving birth to an illegitimate baby left on a person, who wished to keep her own secrets. She was from a more affluent family who knew that if the truth emerged, she would be damned in Victorian society of the time. She threatened suicide if her name was brought into the inquest, which was held on the death of her young daughter. Both these two baby farmers managed to escape any punishment for their crimes, although they were castigated for their lack of care of the children they were supposed to have looked after.

The first case came to light when an inquest was held by Coroner Mr John Humphries on the death of a four month old baby on 30 December 1867. The child was called Alfred Johnson and the inquest was held at the Crown Tavern, Whitecross Street, St Luke's, London. The baby farmer in this case called herself Mrs Matilda Thorne and she lived in one room at Regent Street, City Road, London. She paid 3s 6d a week rent and admitted to the jury that she made her living by taking in children to nurse, and had been engaged in that occupation for over a year. Mr Humphries asked her to describe how the little boy had died. Thorne told him that on Christmas morning at 3 am she was awoken by the child crying and found that he was unwell. She told the inquest that she had kept the child in her arms until 6 am when she took it to the mother's address. Thorne found that Mrs Johnson was not in, but by then the child was quite dead. When she was asked by the Coroner why she had taken the child to the mother's house instead of calling for medical help herself, she told him that Mrs Johnson had a doctor, who had already treated the child once before. When Thorne realised that the mother was not in she brought the baby back to her room and sent for Dr Steadman. She claimed that the child had been ailing a little on Christmas Eve, but it was not ill enough to call out a doctor, as 'I always do when the children get ill'. When Mr Humphries accused her of being a baby farmer, Mrs Thorne was quite indignant. She claimed never to have more than three children at a time, as she found it hard to deal with any more, having already one little boy of her own. She claimed that she had fed the child well on Robb's biscuits and milk and the top crusts from loaves of bread, a diet most unsuitable for a four month old baby. She told the inquest that as widow she had no other means to earn a living, apart from taking in children to support herself and her son.

Thorne claimed that she had always nursed children and had never adopted a child and had no intention of adopting one. The woman told the Coroner that one of the children she looked after was not illegitimate but had a mother and father who pay her 6s a week, but she confessed that most of her other charges were illegitimate. Another child she looked after was that of a servant girl, who paid 5s a week for it. The foreman of the jury said that whatever Thorne might wish to do with regard to the children, it was clear that the system of baby farming was a bad one. By her own admission she had to support herself and her son and three or four other children, and pay the rent out of 15s or £1 a week that she was paid to look after the infants. It was clear that somebody must suffer, for she could not support all the children and herself on such a pittance. When Mr Humphries challenged Mrs Thorne that three other children had already died at her hands, she told him that one child had been brought to her already in a dying state, and it died two months later. With the other she had advertised for a baby, and a lady and gentleman came and asked as favour if the woman could give birth at her premises, which she did. The child was born alive, but it died a month or so afterwards. Mrs Thorne replied that she had only had Alfred, who was four month old, for a fortnight before he died. Dr Steadman then gave his evidence and he said that he had attended to the dead child on Christmas Day at 10 am where he found the baby had been 'long dead'. During the post mortem he noted that there were no marks of violence on the body, although the baby was very emaciated and neglected. He gave the cause of death as congestion of the lungs, brought on by lack of care. The Coroner asked him how long he had known Mrs Thorne to which he replied that he had known her for about six months. He gave the opinion that as far as he could tell she was a careful, respectable woman who attended to the children as well as she could.

Mrs Mary Ann Johnson the deceased child's mother then gave her evidence. She told Mr Humphries that having little money, she was forced to work for a living at a paper bag making. Mrs Johnson told the jury at first that she was married and her husband was stationed in Ireland, but after questioning, admitted that they were not married and therefore the child was illegitimate. When she did not work she only had 7s from the father to keep herself and the baby, and as a consequence had been forced to find some employment making paper bags. The Coroner asked Mrs Johnson how much she made and she replied that she could earn 12s a week if she worked all day until 10 or 12 o'clock at night. Out of that she paid 5s a week for the child at Mrs Thorne's and she still had to find 2s.3d for rent. The remainder of 4s.9d was all she had to keep herself. The witness started to sob as she told the Coroner that:

'I have often lived upon a penny roll and had nothing else to eat for the rest of the day. I did that because I have to support my child. I could not support myself and my child on 7s a week'.

When she saw Mrs Thorne's advert in the *Clerkenwell News*, she took Alfred to her to look after and agreed to visit him once a week. The Coroner in his summing up for the jury, indicated his sympathy for women with illegitimate children in such circumstances, and unusually, he cleared Mrs Johnson of all blame. However he said that although the surgeon had stated that the deceased child had died from congestion of the lungs, a child in that state would require extra care. He claimed that due to the fact that there were four other children in the same room, that the deceased child had only received one fifth of the attention that it ought to have. The jury only consulted for a short while before bringing in a verdict that 'the child died from congestion of the lungs, from want of natural nourishment and care on the part of Mrs Thorne, she having four other children to attend to'. The jury recommended that the whole system of baby farming should be looked into, and urged the Coroner to bring the matter brought before the Home Secretary with a summary of the evidence in the case of this child.

The second case which unfolded the same year, illustrates that was not just working class girls who were seduced and then left to deal with the unwanted pregnancy. Sometimes even affluent mothers could be taken in by these monsters. In many cases when the mother did not visit the child regularly, the only way in which she heard about the death was in the local newspapers. One such woman who had been described as being 'a lady belonging to a wealthy family at Liverpool' was reading her newspaper on Tuesday 24 September 1867. Inside she found a description of the death of a child who had been placed with a baby farmer called Mrs Caroline Jagger of Wood Lane Grove, Tottenham when to her horror realised that it was her own child. The woman had placed her illegitimate baby with Mrs Jagger following an advert, and so she could not believe her eyes when she read the details of the inquest on Mary Stevens aged 1 year and 8 months. The inquest had been held at the Victoria Tavern, Hanger Lane at Tottenham by the Middlesex Coroner, who was again, Mr John Humphries. Identification had been made at the first inquest, and then the case had been adjourned in order that more enquiries could be made by the police. The mother of the child, who called herself Mrs Stevens, had arranged that all the details of the transaction with Jagger had been done through a London solicitors clerk, a Mr Baines. After reading an account of the inquest, the woman contacted the solicitor's clerk and told him of the proceedings. She frantically informed him that if the news that she was the mother of the deceased child came to be known in Liverpool, she would kill herself. By that time the police had discovered that Mr Baines was the solicitor's clerk concerned, and he was summoned to attend the re-convened inquest.

Mr Baines told the Coroner that it was he that had answered the newspaper advert from Mrs Jagger and had made the arrangement for the child to be taken to the woman. When he was asked for the address of 'Mrs Stevens' he told the Coroner that he could not divulge it. The following conversation ensued:

Coroner: Where does Mrs Stevens live?
Baines: I would rather not say
Coroner: I have a public duty to perform. I have to furnish the registrar with a name.
Mr Baines: If I give the name there will be another inquest. The child is illegitimate and the lady has told me that if her name is divulged, she will not return home. You know now my reason. I know what will happen
Coroner: If the jury like, they can let you write the name on paper, and it can be given to me only, and I shall not disclose it.
The witness remained silent.

All he could tell Mr Humphries was that the mother of the child had visited the house owned by Mrs Jagger, and she had brought the four month old little girl with her. Mr Baines had arranged with Mrs Jagger to pay her 6s a week for the girl's maintenance, which he paid her in postage stamps. The child had been registered when it was born, but the mother had only seen it twice since its birth, and the last time had been about four months previously. The child Mary Stephens had lived with Mrs Jagger for one year and four months. Jagger was simply described as 'a married, middle aged woman' and when she appeared at the inquest, she was accompanied by her own solicitor Mr Williams. She told the Coroner that she had looked after the child carefully and that she had eaten well whilst living with her. In answer to a question from a juror, she told him that the kind of food she had given the child included bread, milk, raw eggs and port wine. Not surprisingly with such an inappropriate diet, she stated that the little girl had always been a 'sickly child'. Mrs Jagger claimed that although the child had eaten well, she had vomited a lot, even when Mrs Jagger herself had suckled the child for two months. Her evidence however was negated by the next witness. Surgeon Mr W F Watson who stated that he was a doctor, and had been called in to see the little girl on Thursday 19 September and he had noted that the child was very emaciated. After she had died, he had undertaken the post mortem. He found that the child's stomach was empty and there was no trace of fat on the body, although he had found some disease in the mesenteric glands, which he put down to the fact that the child been badly fed. He told Mr Humphries that he was called to the house again two days later, in order to attend other children, when he was told, almost in an off hand manner, that 'the little girl Mary had died'. He also said that Mrs Jagger had been told by other doctors in the area, not to call them as she had not paid their fees, and on one occasion she had been forced to take a poorly child to a German hospital for treatment.

The Coroner at that point told him to stand down and he recalled Mrs Jagger back into the room. As the magistrate's clerk left to bring her into the room, it was filled by the sounds of a woman screaming loudly. No doubt at that point, Mrs Jagger, fearing the same conclusion as that of the recent case of Mrs Winsor, was terrified for her life. At this point the Coroner who had enough of the woman's performance told her 'isn't it true that I have attended two inquests from children that had died at your house named Adams and Osborn?' After prevaricating for some time, Mrs Jagger finally agreed that was true. He asked her how many children she had through her hands and she admitted to about 40. She was asked by a member of the jury how many children she had at her house at that present time, and she admitted to six adding 'and two little dears that I will never part with. They are two that must be taken care of'. Mr Humphries then asked her if she had any more children upstairs 'that are never seen' and the court was amazed by her screams once more, and cries of 'oh God do not believe that of me'. She continued to shriek in a piercing manner, as she placed her hands over her face. Her solicitor Mr Williams told her sternly to answer the question, and now sobbing and visibly shaking she told him that she hadn't any more children other than those she had told the jury about.

A woman who had called herself Mrs Osborn was then brought into the room, and she gave evidence that she was a cleaner at the house of Mrs Jagger. The woman remembered the little girl called Stevens being brought to the house, and stated that as far as she was concerned the little girl had been attended to well. Jagger's husband then gave his evidence and he told the Coroner that he was aware that his wife had nursed children and that she advertised for them. He told the inquest that Mary Stevens had always been a delicate child from the moment she arrived. The jury retired to debate their verdict and when they returned half an hour later, they told the Coroner that the name of the mother and father of Mary Stevens would not need to be divulged. Surprisingly they found that Jagger was not guilty and that the child had died through disease of the glands, but stated that 'Mrs Jagger is highly censorable for not calling in a medical man to the deceased, and also for the manner in which she had given evidence before the court'. The *Daily Post* later stated that the solicitor Mr Baines had told them that he had merely acted as the go between for 'a young lady of wealth'. She had gone to him for help in his position, which he had held for some years with the family. She had also intimated to him that 'if her name should be divulged, that sooner than live to be ruined for ever, she would commit suicide'. Nevertheless the status of the child's mother made no impression on the way in which the poor child had died.

A curious end-note to this case was provided a few months later in January 1868 when a unnamed child 'aged over three years' was found in a Marylebone workhouse, who was thought to be one of Mrs Jagger's 'children'. It seems that his role was as 'a baby ganger' and he was forced to sit up in the middle of the bed, with as many as eight children around him. At the moment that any of them awoke and started to cry, he had to put a bottle in its mouth. Even at his young age he was also expected to keep the other children quiet and superintend them. He told the workhouse authorities that 'older babies' were put in a box to sleep when 'new babies' brought to 'Mother Jagger'. When he was not attending to the other children, he was tied in a chair as he was unable to walk. He related a day when Mother Jagger had a drop of gin and he, strapped in the chair, fell into the fire. His pinafore caught fire and burnt four fingers off one hand and partially destroyed the muscles of the other hand. It was commented that this young man would never be able to earn his own living, due to his disabilities, and that consequently he had ended up in the workhouse.

Chapter Four: Annie Cummings

The most horrific thing about the baby farming epidemic was the way in which they callously rid themselves of children they no longer thought were profitable. Some poisoned them with narcotics, others fed them unsuitable food whilst many simply abandoned them to die. This particular cowardly way of killing children was popular, because in the majority of cases, the baby farmers were unlikely to be traced and prosecuted. In October 1869 an article pointed out the prevalence of the number of babies found abandoned in the streets around the Fulham and Hammersmith areas of London. The crime was blamed on 'the many baby farmers that were active in that area'. It was reported that:

'the bodies of five children had been found in the neighbourhood around Parson's Green since April, twelve more had been found in Kensington since the previous January and several others in found abandoned in the area of Chelsea'.

It seems that some of the children had been found dead, and others so near to death as they could be. The article sadly warned that the battle against the baby farmers was being lost, concluding that 'by abandoning the babies in this ruthless manner, the baby farmers contrive after all to beat us'.

In February of 1869 a Chelsea lodging house keeper named Mrs Mary Eagle took in a 25 year old woman named Annie Cummings. She had with her, a young boy who was between three and four years of age, who she said was her son and a man who said he was her husband. The couple lodged at the house on Rectory Place, Chelsea for some time. Although there was no obvious sign that she was pregnant, on the 11 April 1869 Mrs Eagle found Cummings in bed with a baby girl. The lodger stated that she had been confined of the child on the previous night, but Mrs Eagle did not believe her and thought the 'newborn' child was in reality a few months old. Cummings told her that she had a friend, a woman called Wood who acted as the midwife and who had attended to her during the night. Unfortunately she had been forced to leave early, as she was indisposed. Mrs Eagle had strong doubts, as she remembered that on the day before her lodger was supposed to have gone into labour, she had eaten a hearty dinner of roast lamb, vegetables and potatoes. She thought this was hardly the actions of a woman in the throes of labour, however despite her suspicions she did nothing. A young girl, Mary Elizabeth Jackson was employed as a nurse for the baby. During the few weeks she looked after the little girl she noted that the baby had the habit of curling up the toes of one foot, and that it had caught thrush. During her employment, Cummings had told Jackson that she was going to send the child into the country, but she never mentioned the name or relationship of the person who was going to take the child.

Cummings told the landlady Mrs Eagle that she had been unable to suckle the child, and as Mrs Eagle kept goats, she offered her some goat's milk for the baby. Although the two women were polite to one another, Mrs Eagle's suspicions continued and she was so convinced that her lodger was a baby farmer that on 21 June she told her to leave. Annie Cummings, did leave as requested, but she took up lodgings next door in the house of neighbour Agnes Burgess. On the night of 5 July 1869, Cummings left the new lodgings taking the baby with her, saying that she was going to meet someone at Chelsea Railway station. She had previously knocked on her landlady's door to tell Mrs Burgess that if her husband should come back in her absence, she was to tell him where she had gone. By now even Mrs Burgess was feeling very suspicious of her lodger, but unlike Mrs Eagle she decided to take action. Telling the little nurse Mary Jackson of her suspicions, they both went out and headed towards Chelsea railway station, but they saw no sign of Cummings or the baby. At 11.15 pm her lodger returned back to the house alone and when Mr Burgess asked her where the baby was, Cummings became emotional and refused to tell him, asking him only 'do you think I do not feel the child going away'. Her suspicious behaviour only confirmed to the landlady that her lodger was one of the hated baby farmers. What she didn't know was that at some time later that same night a boy called Henry Cleverty was passing along 10 Gloucester Road, Brompton, Kensington when he spotted a bundle in the doorway. He picked it up and found a female child wrapped up in a nightgown and a piece of old flannel. At that moment Police Sergeant Henry Troughton came into the street and Cleverty handed the infant over to him, and he took the baby to the Kensington workhouse.

The sergeant reported the incident to his superior officer and he was instructed to make enquiries in the local area. He quickly found that a woman had stayed at lodgings of Mrs Eagle where, it was reported, that she had supposedly given birth to a baby girl. When he questioned Mrs Eagle she told him of her suspicions and how the woman had acted in 'a mysterious manner' on the night of 5 July. He then took Mrs Eagle to the Kensington workhouse, where she correctly picked out the infant that had been abandoned, as the one her lodger had previously had with her. The young nurse Jackson also correctly identified the child she had cared for over the last two weeks. PS Troughton learned that the woman Cummings had moved yet again and was now living at Highfield Road, Brompton. He lost no time in visiting her there. She identified herself as Mrs Cummings and he asked her if she had registered the birth of a child called Ellen May Cummings. She agreed that she had registered the child's birth, and Sergeant Troughton asked to see her, but she told him it was now in Kent. He informed her that an infant had been found abandoned on 5 July and then he arrested her on suspicion of exposing the child, thereby endangering its life, to which she made no reply. He took her into custody where she was searched by a female searcher who found two letters on her. One was addressed to a person with just the initials Y O addressed to Bower's Post Office, Holborn, written on the front of the envelope were the words 'to be called for'. The writer stated:

'To Y O - If the writer will meet me at Bishops Road Railway Station, first class waiting room on Thursday or Friday evening, at half past eight you will oblige. Please write at once, that I may get a letter before evening, so as to be on time. It must be this week and no questions will be asked.
Yours etc., A W'

The other letter was addressed to Mrs Palmer, Post Office Kentish Town Road, also 'to be called for'. The letter stated:

*'Madam,
I beg to say I will adopt your little one if my conditions meet your circumstances, namely to give up the baby for life and that a premium of £8 to be given with it. I will fetch it as soon as it is born'.*

Both letters appeared to be in the handwriting of Annie Cummings.

On Wednesday 1 September 1869 she was brought into the Hammersmith Police Court before the magistrate, Mr Payne charged with exposing the child. Cummings was described in one local newspaper as being 'a very peculiar looking woman, who described herself as married'. Mrs Mary Eagle gave evidence that when she first saw the baby at her own house, it did not look like a newly born infant. She claimed that she had since seen the child at the workhouse, and had identified it as the same little girl. Anne Weatherhead, a nurse at the Kensington workhouse then brought the child into the court room. She told the magistrate that the little girl had much improved in health since she had started caring for her. When the baby had been first brought into the workhouse hospital by a police constable, she seemed to be drugged and had slept for nearly a week. So sleepy was the child that in order to feed her, the nurse was forced to shake it vigorously to arouse it sufficiently for it to eat. The child had been very dirty and emaciated when she started to care for it and had thrush which had not been treated. Mr Payne told the jury that other children had been found abandoned in the same area, and that many of them had been found dead. He stated that two more bodies had been found in Fulham, and they had both since died. Mr Payne added that when inquests had been held on these bodies, the jury had no option but to record a verdict of 'wilful murder'. The magistrate stated that under all these circumstances, and from the number of bodies of children found in these districts, that an example should be made of the prisoner. He pointed out that if it was not for the actions of the boy Cleverty, this child might also have died, and if he had the power he would reward the boy himself. The jury found Annie Cummings guilty and she was sent to take her trial at the next assizes.

Annie Cummings was brought into the Middlesex Assizes on Saturday September 25 1869 before Mr Sergeant Cox. Mr Longford was the barrister for the prosecution and Mr Ribton defended the prisoner, who pleaded not guilty. Mr Longford presented the case to the jury and related the facts leading up to the arrest of the prisoner. Mr Ribton contended that the identity of the child was unclear, and that was the principle point the jury would have to consider. He condemned the number of bodies of young children that had been found in the area, and stated that it 'appeared almost as if they were going back to the ancient days of Rome, when parents exposed their weakly children to die'. Mr Ribton reminded the jury that in those days such a crime 'was done under the sanction of the law, unlike the more modern time we live in today'. The defence counsel told the court that he would let the prisoner speak for herself in an account which she had written. The clerk of the court then read out a rambling and most improbable statement. In it Cummings wrote that she had some years before, become acquainted with a woman of middle age and had done some needlework for her, for which she was paid handsomely. If she wrote to the woman, she would address her envelopes to Mrs Baker, Post Office, Waterloo Road as that was the only address she had for her friend. During the time the two women had been friends, Mrs Baker had always urged her to ask for money if she needed it. When Cummings found that she was pregnant, she confided in her friend, who told her that she was a midwife and that she had a house near to Waterloo Road, where she took in ladies prior to their confinement. She was also acquainted with women who wanted children to adopt. Mrs Baker asked her if she wanted to give up her child to adopt, but Cummings told her that she didn't and nothing more was spoken about it.

Her statement continued to describe how on 10 April she was not feeling very well and she asked her friend to lend her £2. Mrs Baker gave her £1 and told her that if she was well enough to meet her at 5 pm she would bring her the other £1. Cummings said that although they had agreed to meet at 5 pm it was nearly 8 pm before the two women met up on Waterloo Road. During the time she was with Mrs Baker, Cummings became ill again. Mrs Baker's niece was with her and they called a cab and went to Fulham. They reached Mrs Eagle's lodging house at 10 pm and she alleged that her baby was born at 11.15 pm the same night. Mrs Baker attended to her friend during the birth, but left her niece in charge after the child had been born. A short while later the niece told her that she was ill and she too left the house. Cummings statement described how her husband at that time was working and earning about 16s a week, out of which she had to provide for the two adults and now two children, one aged three years and the other just a few days old. Two weeks after the baby had been born, her husband came out of work and had not worked since. She claimed that she had pledged most of her belongings to buy food. The prisoner stated that she was unable to suckle her own infant due to it 'being an eight month child'. Mrs Eagle had offered her the goats milk, but after a few weeks her landlady told her that the goat did not give enough milk for both families, and refused to let her have any more. When her lodger owed her two weeks rent, Mrs Eagle asked her to leave.

Cummings described moving to the lodgings next door, and shortly afterwards met up with her friend Mrs Baker again. The woman once more asked her to allow her baby to be adopted, and assured her friend that she would be able to see the baby occasionally. Cummings, who described herself as a 'distraught mother' only accepted on the proviso that the little girl would only be given to a couple who were able to give her a good home. Mrs Baker told her that she could buy the baby presents, which her friend would undertake to carry to the child, but only on the understanding that Cummings did not know the address where the baby lived with its new parents. It was finally agreed and the prisoner wrote that she had met Mrs Baker on 5 July where she handed over the baby at 10.15 pm. Cummings told the court that her baby was born with bright blue eyes and fair hair, and the child that she had been shown at the Kensington workhouse was dark haired and therefore it was definitely not her child. That was the end of her statement. Cummings told the court that after she had given the baby to Mrs Baker she had received a letter about three weeks later, which she had read out to Mrs Burgess. The letter claimed that the people who had adopted the child were so pleased with the little girl and they hoped that her mother would not want her back. Cummings told the court that Mrs Burgess also knew that she had made some petticoats for the child, and she had also bought a little bonnet for the baby for 5s, which she had given to her friend to deliver to the new parents. The prisoner claimed that Sergeant Troughton had also found some other baby articles which she had intended to give her little girl when he was searching the house. Cummings told the court that she was saving to buy the baby a little pelisse and then she was going to send all the articles through Mrs Baker. She stated that 'if I did not expect to see my baby again, or if I thought it was not a good home, I should not prepare these little things to send her'.

Cummings said that the two letters that had been on her person when she was arrested, had been written in her own hand. The letters were responses to letters sent to Mrs Baker, from a woman wanting a baby to adopt. Mrs Baker was unable to write and therefore she wrote letters for her and Mrs Baker paid her a few shillings for this service, which she badly needed. Cummings stated that for two or three weeks she had told both Mrs Burgess and the girl Jackson, that the baby was going to be sent away, although she admitted that she did not tell them that the baby was to be adopted. Cummings stated that she never told other people about her troubles, but she had always tried to bring her children up as respectable. The man that the prisoner had been living with next took the stand, and stated his name to be Charles Robert Cummings and that he was a gardener by trade. He told the court that he and the prisoner were not married, but that he had lived with her for the past nine months. He said that she had been delivered of a baby in April last, and the child lived with them for two months or more. Mr Cummings told the court how the infant had been sent away on 5 July and that the child that had been produced at the police court was not the same one. He confirmed that he knew the baby was going to be adopted by a couple who lived in the country, and although he had never met Mrs Baker, he confirmed that the prisoner had talked about her many times. However his story was found to be untrue in the many of the main points. When the man was cross examination by Mr Longford for the prosecution, he admitted that he had not actually seen the child being born, and that Annie Cummings had never told him that she was giving the baby to Mrs Baker,

In his summing up the prosecution, Mr Longford immediately cast doubt on the evidence of Mr Cummings, and alluded to the fact that he was well know to the police having indulged in 'matters of a more nefarious nature'. He also questioned that if such a person as Mrs Baker had existed 'whose only address was the Post Office on Waterloo Road' then why had she not come forward to give evidence to the court on her friends behalf. Mr Longford stated categorically that he strongly believed that no such person had ever existed. He asserted that if that were true, therefore the case for the prosecution of the prisoner was fully made out against her. Mr Sergeant Cox summed up the evidence and the jury retired to consider their verdict. After an hours absence they returned back into the court and returned a verdict of guilty. The sentence upon Annie Cummings was that she was to be kept in penal servitude for five years and she seemed to be indifferent to her fate as she was led out of the dock.

Shocking though the details of this case appear, it was only the beginnings of the baby farming revelations which were to be brought before the newspaper reading public. A year later the *Pall Mall Gazette* of 21 June 1870 announced that the number of bodies that had be found in the area, before and after the trial could be clearly attributed to the prisoner Annie Cummings. Police investigations had established that she was supposed to have been employed by one or more of the less squeamish baby farmers in the area, to 'dispose' of the bodies of their victims on the streets and alleyways of London. It therefore cannot be ignored that there were operating several baby farms in the area, which the police authorities were unable to close down. But the next case proved that the women like Annie Cummings were just minor players, in what was to become, the most shocking crime in the annals of Victorian history.

Chapter Five: Margaret Waters and Sarah Ellis.

Of all the baby farmers I have researched, I have to say that this case is one of the most callous. Margaret Waters was just one of only three women in this book to be hanged, and in my opinion she truly deserved her fate. At the time this crime was committed, the increasing numbers of dead bodies of children found on the streets, left the people of Britain clamoring for the government to bring out some legislation to stop these terrible deaths. Thankfully the diligence of an officer of the Brixton Police Force was instrumental in bringing these two criminals to justice. Like all the women in this book, the true numbers of children they disposed of will never be known, but this case even rivaled that of the woman who came to epitomize baby farmers, serial killer Amelia Dyer. This case also shows the increasing use of drugs by baby farmers, used not only to quieten the children but at the same time to suppress their appetite. Because the trade of baby farming had been so reviled in the newspaper press, these women cunningly kept the knowledge that they was caring for more than one child away from the parents.

In 1844 Margaret and Sarah Forth were born and brought up in Bingley, near Leeds. At the time it would seem that Margaret Waters was the most unlikely person to take up her future career. She was supposed to be a young woman of great intelligence, who in 1863 was respectably married to a man who was described as 'being in good circumstances'. When Waters husband died in Glasgow a few years later, he left her £300 which she used to set herself up in business. She moved from Glasgow and rented a house in Addington Square, Camberwell. At first Waters wanted to set up in business for herself, so she bought a number of sewing machines and employed staff to make collars for sale to city people. However she did not having a head for business, which resulted in the first year of a loss of £250. But Waters was a resourceful woman, and soon decided on letting out part of her premises as lodgings. It was said that one of her first lodgers was a woman with a child, who was the mistress of a city solicitor. The unnamed woman offered Waters money to nurse the child for her, and soon word spread, and eventually she found herself taking care of three more children. It was at this point that Waters began the slide down into poverty and embraced her career as baby farmer. Financial matters declined once again and she was forced to move to a slightly less respectable neighbourhood, and was obliged to borrow from a money lender at a large rate of interest. In an attempt to provide a motive for her horrific deeds, it was said that that her concerns about money drove this 'debt ridden woman to become callous to the real nature of the crimes she was about to commit'.

However research proves that the biggest turning point was when her father died insane in 1867, and her mother came to live with her. The old lady objected to having children in the house, and that was when Waters caught onto the idea used by many women before her. She would adopt children for £10 and put the children out to nurse at a lower cost. Like many others before her, Waters would meet the woman who agreed to nurse the child, she would offer a small weekly price and hand over two weeks money in advance. Waters soon discovered that very rarely was she asked for an address or contact details. At that point she would simply disappear and without shame would pocket the difference. During the height of the police investigations a woman called Mrs Carter came forward and explained how she had been given a baby in September 1867 to care for by Waters who had told her that 'a fashionable dressed woman' had brought the baby to her in August or September of that year. Mrs Carter had agreed to look after the child for 7s a week, but after offering her two weeks in advance she never saw Waters again. No doubt by such a scheme Waters thought she would make her fortune, but once again she quickly found herself in more debt, and was forced to borrow £28 from a notorious money lender against her furniture. Waters later told the police that the man was well known in the area, stated that he charged her £14 expenses, and in order to keep her furniture and evade his clutches, she was obliged to move several times. At some point her mother disappeared and her sister Sarah Ellis joined her, and it was at that point that Waters and Ellis started their infamous career. In her confession she claimed that up to that point she had always cared for the children when they were ill, and she would call in a doctor. If they died, she would usually paid out a small amount to an undertaker in order to have them buried, but when she moved to the house in Brixton, a total of five children died on her. Waters claimed that some of them had died from diarrhea, and others from a wasting disease which doctors called 'a failure to thrive'. However both were symptoms that the child had been neglected. Not surprisingly at that time Waters was once again in financial straits, and decided to save the small amount of money on burials, by leaving the children's bodies out in the street. Only much later did she admit that perhaps another four children had been disposed of in the exactly same manner.

To begin with Waters developed a foolproof scheme of ensuring that she was not responsible for abandoning the unwanted adopted child. In her confession, Waters admitted that at this time she would take the baby out and find a group of children playing in the streets. She would offer one of the children a sixpence to hold her baby for her, whilst she went to a sweetshop to get them some sweets and then would make off. Waters usually found these abandoned children were sent to the workhouse. In her confession Waters admitted watching one little boy who held the baby she had given him, and when she did not return, the boy himself began to cry. She had disappeared into an oyster shop and when the young boy became disturbed, a policeman was called. He took the boy and the baby away, whilst Waters quickly made her escape. However soon she changed her tactics and simply abandoned the child in the streets. Later police enquiries found that the two sisters had moved house and changed their names several times. Whilst they were living at Battersea bodies of children turned up everywhere. A dead body of a child was found in St George's Terrace, and another child found alive in St George's Road, Battersea. The prevalence of dead bodies and the inability to do anything about it, was beginning to disturb legal authorities.

About this time a woman called Mary Ann Grainge of St John's Wood contacted Waters. She had a sister called Elizabeth Still who had been delivered of an illegitimate child on 22 December 1869 and four days later Mrs Grainge saw an advertisement offering to adopt a child. She replied and soon afterwards met Waters, who said that her name was Florence Watson. An arrangement was made for Watson to visit Mrs Grainge and Elizabeth at the house in St John's Wood and she was shown the baby. She said that she and her husband were very fond of children, but at that time Elizabeth was unwilling to part with the child, and Mrs Grainge wrote to Watson to let her know in a letter addressed to Deacons Newsroom's on Leadenhall Street. She had asked Watson for her address, but the woman replied she said that she was unable to give it to her as her husband would object. Mrs Grainge received this letter in reply:

'Dear Madam - I cannot say how sorry I am that you decline to let us have your baby. We have as I told you, a nice home and every comfort, and are very fond of children. Why we so much desire a young child is that it may know no other love than ours, and always look upon us as its parents. We are not unmindful of the heavy responsibility we incur in adopting a baby as our own, and in doing so should strictly consider it's happiness and comfort, and promise that its future should be well provided for. Should you think more of this, we shall be very pleased to hear from you, for I just long for a little one as that is our want, our only wish,
Yours respectfully FLORENCE WATSON*

Reluctant as always to let a baby go, on the 5 January 1870 the woman Mrs Grainge knew as Watson came to her house again, and begged once more to be able to take the child. Her sister finally agreed and asked if she could go home with Watson as she was unhappy about surrendering her child to a complete stranger. The woman told Mrs Grainge that if she wanted a reference, she could contact Mrs Ellis of Bournemouth Road, Peckham. The same night Mrs Grainge received another letter from Watson saying that her husband would not object to her adopting the baby 'but that when we take it, we do so for ever'. As a result of the letter, Mrs Grainge went to see Mrs Ellis at the address she had been given for a reference, not knowing that it was in fact Water's own sister. Mrs Ellis told her that the child 'will have a good home with Mrs Watson'. The next day she agreed for Watson to adopt the child and she gave her the £2. She never saw the baby again.

Still more little bodies were being found in the streets around Brixton. On Saturday 1 January 1870 the body of a dead, female child was found in Holly Street, by a man cleaning out the ash pits in an open yard. He called a police constable who told him to take the body to the police station. There the police surgeon established that the body was about a week old and it had been covered in ashes. Whether this was in an attempt to hide the body or accidental, it could not be determined. There was only two houses standing in the yard itself, but there was plenty of access into the yard from the street. The constable had made enquiries from the two nearest houses, but no one who lived in the neighbourhood knew anything about a child being born, or of a mother giving birth. At the subsequent inquest the Coroner told the jury:

'you seldom hear of children being thrown into ashpits near the house of their parents; they generally come from a distance. I think we shall not hear any more of this and we had better return an open verdict'.

The Coroner was correct and the jury dutifully returned a verdict of 'found dead'. Only later did the real truth emerge.

At this point the adverts for baby farmers were becoming such a nuisance that the police authorities were determined to stamp out this vile trade where possible. The Brixton Police Force were aware of the large numbers of dead babies that had been found on their patch, as many of them had been found by their own officers. Police Constable King reported to his superiors that he had found the body of a female baby on 10 May on Brunswick Road, lying under a hedge close to the footpath. The little body was covered with a napkin and blue paper, tied up with string. The following week a labourer Reuben Frederick Francis was going to work when he found the body of a male child on 17 May behind an old signboard in Mead Lane, Brixton, once again tied up in brown paper. Another officer, Police Constable Alford stated that he had found a body of a male child in a basket which had been covered over by a brown rug on 26 May about 5 am. The body, which was very decomposed, had been wrapped in an old and ragged woman's nightgown. On 6 June on the very same premises the constable found another little body wrapped in brown paper parcel. Once again he found it in the early hours of the morning. He reported to his superiors that it was about 3.30 am when he found it, under some black stuff and pieces of red flannel. Inside the parcel was the body of a female child aged about 5 or 6 weeks of age.

One of the officers of the Brixton Police Force was most determined to do something about these cases of abandoned babies, which they knew had been dumped by a baby farmer. His name was Police Sergeant Richard Relf and he decided to keep a look out for places where they might be caught. He had been on duty on Saturday 28 May 1870 in Camberwell Road shortly after 10 am when he saw a four wheeled cab draw up outside the house of a midwife called Mrs Barton. It was strongly suspected that she kept a lying-in house and so he watched the proceedings with interest. An elderly woman got out of the cab and went inside the house. Shortly afterwards she came out again with a delicate looking female, who he afterwards learned was Miss Jeanette Tassy Cohen. He followed the cab to a house in Loughborough Road, which was a very respectable district. Relf made enquiries and found that during her stay at Camberwell Road, Miss Cohen had given birth to a boy on 14 May, who she had named John Walter Cohen. The child had been handed over to a woman, known only as Mrs Willis, at a house on Frederick Terrace on 18 May. The elderly woman had been Miss Cohen's mother who had gone to bring her daughter home. Relf searched the registers in a nearby church of St Giles, and found that an illegitimate child named Cohen had been registered there. Armed with this information Relf went to Loughborough Road, Brixton and spoke to the girl, and she told him that she had indeed given birth to a child and that her father had made the arrangements with Mrs Willis for the child to be adopted for £5. Miss Cohen's father told the sergeant that he had seen the advertisement to adopt in *Lloyds Weekly Newspaper* dated 1 May 1870 and had contacted Mrs Willis through that. Despite extensive enquiries no one knew anything about Mrs Willis or had an address for her. He had looked at all the people living on Frederick Terrace, but there was no Mr or Mrs Willis to be found.

Most people would have given up at this point, but Sergeant Relf was made of sterner stuff. He decided to keep an eye on these advertisements and a few days later he saw one dated June 5 signed by a Mrs Oliver. When he reported it to his superior officer, he had noted that now the adverts asking for children to adopt used the code 'entirely adopted' and 'includes everything'. The advert said:

'Adoption - a good home with a mothers love and care, is offered to any respectable person wishing her child to be entirely adopted. Premium £5, which sum includes everything. Apply by letter only Mrs Oliver, the Post Office, Grove Place, Brixton'

Relf corresponded with 'Mrs Oliver', who he later found to be the woman called Sarah Ellis who appeared to be about 29 years of age. Also using a false name and dressed in plain clothes, Relf agreed to meet her at Camberwell New Road Railway Station on 11 June, where he spoke to her about taking his fictitious child to adopt. Ellis told him that she had been married for thirteen years and had no family of her own. The woman told him that 'if he entrusted his child with her, it would receive a mothers love and a good education'. Relf thought that she seemed very anxious to get the boy and also to get away from him. According to his instructions from his superiors, Relf followed Ellis when she left the station and he was delighted to see her enter a house on Frederick Terrace. The next night Sunday 11 June at 9 pm he went to the house on Frederick Terrace and knocked on the door. It was answered by a woman who said her name was Margaret Waters who he judged to be about 35 years. Relf asked if Mrs Willis was there, but she told him there was no one of that name at the house. He introduced himself as a police sergeant, and informed her that he had for many months been observing the comings and goings at the house and he knew that it was being used as a baby farming establishment. The woman hotly denied it and Relf then went to the address of Miss Cohen and told her that he thought he had found out where her baby was being held. Accompanied by Miss Cohen's father, Mr Robert Tassy Cohen, the two men went back to the house on Frederick Terrace and demanded to see Miss Cohen's baby. Mrs Waters told them indignantly that they certainly did not adopt babies. Relf insisted that they intended to see the child, and that he was not leaving until they did. Eventually the woman he knew as Oliver came to the door with the child in her arms. Relf and Mr Cohen were disgusted as the child appeared to be merely skin and bone, was in a filthy condition and wrapped in rags.

Mr Cohen stated that when the child was born, it had been strong and healthy and he barely recognized it as the same child that had been handed over. Relf insisted on searching the premises and he strode into the kitchen, which was at the front of the house. There he found another five infants all aged less than a month old, and they all appeared sleepy as they lay together on a sofa. Their little bodies were all huddled together for warmth, and they were covered with different types of dirty clothing. All of them were filthy and emaciated, and two of them appeared to be in a dying, moribund condition. In the back yard Sergeant Relf found five more older children playing, they were aged from 14 months to 2 years, and appeared to be in a slightly better condition. Waters said that she was paid a weekly fee for these children, before admitting that she had been in the 'nursing' business for four years. When Relf asked her how many children had she looked after in total, she told him that she had about forty children under her charge. Waters said that all the children were illegitimate, and she did not know where the mothers lived. Relf guessed that at least one of the children appeared to be under the effects of a narcotic, and this was confirmed when he found a bottle labelled 'Paregoric Elixir' which contained a preparation of opium and other drugs. Upstairs a further five infants were found. The use of such preparations was common in Victorian London and were recklessly used on children particularly when teething, or to give a mother a good nights sleep. It was not only given to the children to suppress appetite and keep them quiet. It was found that Amelia Dyer herself addicted herself to laudanum, which was easily obtainable over the counter from chemist shops. Perhaps baby farmers used it as a coping mechanism, undertaking the kind of work which they did, it might be suggested that they used it to try to distance themselves from the horror of their lives.

Edward Pope a local surgeon was hastily summoned, and he examined all the children and he too was appalled at the dirty condition of the house. The infants ages ranged from three weeks to three months old. One of the children that looked about three weeks old had a feeding bottle with some cornflour and water in it, which the surgeon knew was totally unfit for a child of that age. Another small child did have a bottle with some milk in it, which was sour. The surgeon told Relf that there was little chance of the children surviving with the food that he found in the house. He ordered that all the children were to be immediately sent to the Lambeth workhouse to be cared for. Pope knew from his quick examination of the children, that at least two of them were in a critical condition and were not expected to live. All of them were suffering from the effects of starvation to a different degree. The child belonging to Miss Cohen was given to a wet nurse and the two women were taken into custody. When the house on Frederick Terrace was being more thoroughly searched, officers found a total of 30 letters which had been written and received by mothers of some of the children. The police immediately started an investigation into each and every one. When Waters had arrived at the Brixton police station, she was arrested and searched, and £11 in gold was found on her person, as well as 79 pawn tickets and twelve more letters from mothers wishing to have their child 'adopted'.

On Monday 13 June 1870 at the Lambeth Police Court, Margaret Waters and Sarah Ellis were charged with neglecting to provide proper food and nourishment for the male child of Jeanette Tassy Cohen. The magistrate Mr Elliott told the court that although ten children had been found at the house, the two women were being charged with regard to four other children in their possession. Although their names were unknown, Waters and Ellis were also charged with not providing enough food and nourishment for them too. Present at the court was Mr Moore for the Protection of Women and Children and Captain Baines watched the case on behalf of the police authorities. When the prisoners appeared in court they looked to be about to faint, and so were allowed to be seated. The prisoner Waters had a child in her arms in the courtroom, which she stated was her own, although the child was very small and 'appeared to be suffering'. The waiting room of the court had temporarily been turned into a nursery, as police officers wives cared for the 10 children there. Sergeant Relf told the magistrate that when Ellis was arrested, Margaret Waters said to him 'believe me what my sister did was under my direction, I am the guilty one and I must suffer'. Miss Cohen's baby was produced in court, and its terrible condition caused a sensation amongst those present. Mrs Ann Rowland appeared in the court and told the magistrates that she had taken charge of the baby, but it was so ill and wasted to nothing and she feared that it might not survive. The magistrate remanded the prisoners for a further week, and the children were sent back to the workhouse to be nursed and fed.

On the day that Relf had visited the house on Frederick Terrace and taken them into custody, the bodies of two more infants had been found. On Tuesday 14 June 1870 an inquest was held on these bodies by Coroner Mr Carter at the Marlborough Arms Tavern, South Street, Camberwell. Acting Inspector Hammond watched the case on behalf of the police. He told the Coroner that over the previous few weeks, that no less than 16 bodies of dead infants had been found in the immediate locality of Brixton. A young lad named George Anderson gave evidence that he had found the body of a little girl which had been wrapped in blue cloth under some logs on Sunday 12 June. The police surgeon, Mr Dawson stated that the body was terribly decomposed, showing that it had been kept somewhere for quite a while, before being dumped. This was a favourite method which was later used by Amelia Dyer, who kept the bodies for a few weeks, hopping that decomposition would prevent any detection. The method worked in so far that surgeon, Mr Dawson told the Coroner that it was impossible to say what had caused the death of the child. He was able to state however that it was a fully developed child, which appeared to be just a few months old. The body was also wrapped in brown paper and most damningly written on the paper was the name 'Mrs Waters'. This was another parallel with the capture of Amelia Dyer twenty six years later. She too left a body wrapped in a brown paper parcel, which contained the name and address at which she was at that time living. The Coroner asked Inspector Hammond if it was connected with the [Waters] case at present being investigated, but the Inspector responded that he was not allowed to say at the moment. The second witness was a lamplighter called Mr George Dean and he said that he had found the second body the previous Sunday under a railway arch at Brixton. Once again it was in a very offensive state owing to decomposition. The body was wrapped in a napkin, fastened with a black band. The whole was then covered in brown paper also with the name 'Waters' written on it. Once again it was difficult to establish exactly how the child had died. Under the direction of the coroner, the jury brought in a verdict that both children had been 'found dead'

On Monday 20 June the two woman were brought once more into the court and the first to give evidence was Mr Robert Tassy Cohen, the father of the girl Jeanette. He told the magistrates that she was his youngest daughter aged just 17 years and that she had given birth to a male child on 14 May. On the 1 May he had seen an advertisement for a baby to adopt in *Lloyds Weekly Newspaper*. An appointment had been made for the 7 May and he met the prisoner Waters in the waiting room of Camberwell Station. She had previously told him her name was Willis, but then denied it saying 'that was the name she used for adoptions'. She told him that her husband was a representative of a large shipping firm, and they had been married for thirteen years without any children of their own. Mr Cohen told her at that time that the child had not yet been born, but admitted that it was illegitimate. Waters told him that made no difference to her. He wrote to her again on the 16 May to say that the child had been born and on Tuesday 17 May Waters called upon him and told him that she would take the child the next day, and he agreed to meet her at Walworth Road station. He and his housekeeper had delivered the child to Waters. On

Sunday 11 June he went with the police to Water's house and saw the state of the child who he had last seen as a healthy and beautiful baby. As he looked with horror on the state of his grandson, he said to her 'My God Mrs Waters, you are murdering this child'. She told him the baby had been ill and 'she had done all in her power for it'. He then told the court that the child had gone to a wet nurse called Mrs Ann Rowland, who had attempted to nurse him, but sadly he had since died.

A servant named Ellen O'Connor, who had been employed by Waters and Ellis, next gave evidence against them. The girl who was aged only 14, told the court that three months ago she had been employed by the two sisters. At the time she was engaged she knew Waters as Mrs Blackburn, and when she first went to the house there were only seven infants there. One of those was Ellis's baby. O'Connor told the court that she only knew three of the others by their first name of Teddy, Joe and Willy. Shortly after she started work for the two sisters, the number of infants increased to eleven. She told the magistrates that some children were 'taken away at night' and when she enquired about them the next morning, she was told that they were ill and had been taken back to their mothers. O'Connor also described to the magistrates how part of her duties involved going the Post Office in Grove Place, Brixton to collect any letters which had been addressed to a Mrs Oliver. The girl said that after Waters read the letters they were generally burned. One of the letters which had been found at the house waiting to be posted, was read out in court. The letter illustrates the devious untruths to which women such as Waters and Ellis would sink to obtain a child. The letter was dated Wednesday June 8 and said:

Sir, In reply to your letter, I beg to say that it would give me great pleasure to adopt as my own, your little boy, if he is not too old. You omitted to state the child's age, and I wish for one as young as possible, that it may know none but ourselves as its parents. The child would be well brought up, and carefully educated. He would have a good trade and be to us in all respects as our own. We have been married several years, but have no family. We are in a comfortable position, have a good business, and a home in every way calculated to make a child happy. We are both very fond of children and should you entrust your little one to my care, you may rely upon his receiving the love and care of a mother. Any place you would like to appoint for an interview will suit me. I can meet you at any time you please, and should be very glad to have the matter settled as soon as possible. Hoping to have an early reply. I am sir, respectfully
Yours. Mrs R OLIVER

The girl continued with her evidence, saying that Waters would often send her to Mr Keys chemist shop in Loughborough Road for laudanum. She was instructed to say that if anyone was to ask what she wanted it for, she was to tell them it was for toothache. Waters also often sent her for lime to a building close by, which she said was to keep the sickness away from the children. She described how she would put a piece of lime, about as big as her hand, into a jug of water and allowing it to stand for an hour. Then a dessertspoon full was put into each infants feeding bottle under Waters direction. She said the children were fed cornflour, milk and water and Dr Ritchie's Patent Food whilst Mrs Ellis fed her own baby with the breast. O'Connor then identified items which had been found with two of the dead infants at Brixton. She told the court that a handkerchiefs which had been found wrapped around one of the bodies, she had last seen at the house of the two sisters. She also recognized the rug which had covered the body of the child which had been found in a basket. She told the magistrate that the rug had previously been used to cover Ellis's baby. A nightgown that had been wrapped around one of the bodies was identical to one seen at the house. Continuing with her evidence, O'Connor remembered about a week earlier Ellis coming home from the meeting with Sergeant Relf, who she later knew had posed as a potential father at the Camberwell Railway Station. Ellis was rather drunk and Waters asked her if she agreed terms with the man, to which her sister told her that she had. Just at that moment the two woman and the girl noted a man looking in at the window. Seeing Relf outside, Waters shouted at her sister 'you nasty cat, you have ruined me'.

The next two witnesses were the workhouse nurses who gave evidence about the state of the other children when they arrived at the Lambeth workhouse, and they reported that two of them had since died. Dr Edward Pope the surgeon described for the magistrates how he found the children at the house when he was summoned to attend by Sergeant Relf. He described find a bottle with laudanum in it, which had been given to Miss Cowan's child. Pope had since completed a post mortem and found that death was caused by atrophy and extreme wasting, which had caused congestion of the brain. He told the court that giving any young child a narcotic, would almost certainly cause those symptoms, and would also interfere with the digestion. The prosecution, Mr Poland made a statement to say at that time that he did not intend to take the case any further, but he hoped that as the police enquiries were continuing, that more woman might come forward, and more evidence gathered against the two prisoners. The magistrate agreed and the case was once more adjourned. Before the court was cleared however, Superintendent Gernon stated that there were several women in the court who wanted to know what had happened to their children. Several females came forward and addressed the two prisoners in the dock asking them 'tell me where my child is?' Waters looked very confused and frightened, but heartlessly she told them nothing, saying merely that 'I will leave it all to my solicitor'. Two of the females gave descriptions of their children, who it was thought were two of the children still in the workhouse. One young woman, who said she had handed her baby over to Waters, begged the prisoners to tell her where her baby was. The two sisters treated her with great contempt, saying 'we shan't tell you anything about it'. Margaret Waters and Sarah Ellis were remanded once again and they were booed and hissed at by the people in the courtroom as they left.

Whilst the two women were being held in custody, more of their dealings were given in the newspapers reports of the time. It was said that once they had been arrested that other women had come forward to the Brixton police station making enquiries as to the fate of their own children, who had been placed with Margaret Waters. It was also reported that one of the children that had been taken to the workhouse, had already been claimed by its mother and given back into her care. Another unnamed woman attended the police station on Wednesday 22 June 1870 stating that she had handed her baby over to the woman, she now believes was Waters. She had given the child for adoption to a woman who told her that her name was Fanny Stewart, for a premium of £4. In return she received a receipt which she showed to the police authorities. It stated:

'March 4 1870

Received the sum of £4, for which I take this child and promise to adopt it entirely as my own, never again to give it up, but always to strictly study its present and future happiness.

FANNY STEWART'

The same woman identified some of the articles of clothing which had been found at the house, as those which had belonged to her child. Sadly despite many diligent police enquiries, no trace of her infant was ever found. On Wednesday 29 June another child's body was found under the arches of the London, Chatham and Dover Railway at Camberwell. The body was found by workmen, and it was wrapped in a bundle of rags. The body was removed to the house on Frederick Terrace, which was about a quarter of a mile away, and several neighbour's and witnesses were asked if they could identify the body from the clothing, but they were unsuccessful.

A second inquest was held on the bodies of John Walter Cohen, and two more of the unknown children, which had been found at the house on Frederick Terrace and which had died at the workhouse. The inquest was heard on Friday July 1 at the Committee Room of the Lambeth workhouse. The jury went to see the three bodies that were still in the hospital, and were visibly shocked at the state of the little emaciated bodies. The woman at whose house Miss Cohen had given birth, Maria Castle told the court that she was used to taking care of women during their confinement. Mr Cohen appeared once again and told the inquest that his daughter's baby was a product of her being 'outraged' by the husband of a woman she had been staying with, and that a warrant was presently out for the man's arrest. The Coroner told the jury that if they believed that Waters or Ellis had really intended to take those children lives, they should bring in a verdict to that effect. He praised the efforts of Sergeant Relf and said that 'but for his energy, this iniquitous business would probably have continued'. The room was then cleared whilst the Coroner remained with the jury. When the doors were opened again, he told them that the jury had brought in a verdict of manslaughter in the case of Miss Cohen's child. However they decided that the cause of death in the other two children was from atrophy, which had been brought on by insufficient food and the continued use of narcotics.

On Wednesday 6 July 1870 Margaret Waters and Sarah Ellis were brought into the magistrates court once again, and Mr Poland informed the bench, that yet another baby had since died at the workhouse. The Medical Officer, Dr Bullen had stated that when the children were brought to the workhouse, and in the absence of names, they had been given numbers. Three children had been identified and taken away by their mothers and the children numbered 6, 8 and 9 had since died. No 9 had been a female child of from four to six months old who had been admitted on the same afternoon as the other children, and she had died the previous day. The surgeon told the magistrate that the child had been in a comatose state for over 12 hours before it died, but that he had been unable to make a post mortem examination until he received the Coroner's Order, which he now had. He said that three children remained, and although one of them was very poorly, two of them might possibly survive. Mary Ann Grainge of St John's Wood then gave her evidence. She described to the court how her sister, Elizabeth had been delivered of an illegitimate child on 22 December 1869. When she saw the case being reported in the newspapers, she had gone to the Lambeth workhouse and although she was horrified at the state of the children there, she could not identify her sister's child. Two more young women came forward and swore that Waters and Ellis had taken their children, and confirmed that they had never seen their children since parting with them. The next witness was another former servant who had worked for Waters and Ellis. Her name was Annie Warden and In January of 1870 she had gone to the house, and Waters had taken her upstairs to show her the dead body of a six week old child known only as Arthur. Waters had said to her 'don't say anything about it'. Warden said that Waters had told her that the boy had died from convulsions the previous Sunday. The witness then told a hushed court that there had been no funeral and she did not know what had became of the little body. At the same time she asked Waters what had become of a little girl called Davis aged three months and James aged four months who she had seen on a previous visit. Waters told her that they had died the previous May, after being with her for only a fortnight. She told her former servant that she had washed the bodies and laid them out, although once again there was no funeral. The prisoners were once again remanded.

On Friday 8 July, a further inquest was held on another child that had died in the Lambeth workhouse. Although the name of the child was not known, the servant girl Ellen O'Connell identified her as Caroline Castle. She told the inquest that she had been fed by a bottle which had milk, cornflour and arrowroot mixed in. Sometimes she was fed with a spoon, when she was unable to take the bottle. The child cried a great deal, but she also slept a good deal too. Mr Bullen again stated that there was no evidence to show where the child had come from. A verdict was brought in that the child died from congestion of the brain, brought on by starvation and the administration of opium. On Wednesday 27 July the two women were brought up before the magistrates again at Lambeth Police Court. Mr Poland stated that out of the eleven children found in the house only one child remained unaccounted for, five had died and three had been claimed by their mothers. The remaining two were Mrs Ellis child who was still alive, and Miss Cohen child who had also died. He reminded the court that a verdict had been brought against Waters of manslaughter, but the question was should she be committed on the more serious charge of wilful murder. The question was did these two women intend to murder the children when they took charge of them, or did they stupidly neglect to give them food. Mr Poland said that there was absolutely no doubt in his mind that both women were equally guilty, although he felt that Waters was the chief culprit. Both women were charged with four counts of murder, manslaughter, conspiracy and obtaining money by false pretences.

Margaret Waters and Sarah Ellis were brought into the dock of the Old Bailey on Tuesday 16 August 1870, now charged with six indictments of murder, to which both prisoners pleaded not guilty. Because some information had come to light which the defence had not yet received, it was asked that the trial be postponed until the next session, which was agreed. On Saturday 24 September 1870 the trial started in front of Chief Baron Kelly and it had been decided that the two women would be tried for the murder of just one child. Consequently both woman were charged with the wilful murder of John Walter Cohen. It was reported that the prisoners had lost much of the levity they had shown at previous examinations, and they now appeared to take their position very seriously indeed. One of the witnesses was a clerk called Thomas Bassett who worked in the advertising section of *Lloyds Weekly Newspaper*. He produced 27 advertisements which had been given to him by the two sisters, who he knew quite well. They had brought in the written advertisements both separately and together, and had paid 5s for each one. By now the witnesses were so numerous that the case was adjourned to the following Monday. Members of the jury were told that they would be accommodated for the night at the Cannon Street Hotel in the charge of an usher of the court.

When the court reconvened on Monday, the judge ordered that there was not enough evidence against Ellis and that she would be found not guilty, but he ordered that she be kept in custody until all the other charges had been investigated. The medical evidence was heard before the defence and prosecution began their closing speeches. Chief Baron Kelly in his summing up stated that the questions the jury had to consider were: was the death of John Walter Cowen caused by the want of sufficient and proper nourishment which the prisoner ought to have supplied. By the administration of laudanum or any other narcotic by the prisoner or by the want of medical attention which the prisoner ought to have supplied. The jury left the room and while they were absent, Sarah Ellis was placed back in the dock. She pleaded guilty to obtaining money by false pretences, and not providing sufficient clothing for the children, as well as conspiracy with Margaret Waters. It was then indicated that the jury was about to return to give their verdict on Margaret Waters, and so Ellis was quickly removed from the dock. In all the jury had taken just 55 minutes before bringing in a verdict that Margaret Waters was guilty of wilful murder. When the prisoner was asked if she had anything to say, she simply made a convoluted statement that there had been much evidence against her that was simply untrue. She blamed the death of the children in the workhouse on the fact that they had been taken from their bed early in the day, and kept at Lambeth police station until the late afternoon. Waters claimed by the time they arrived at the workhouse their clothes were wet and yet she was being blamed for their deaths. She ended by stating that 'I am innocent of these little ones having perished'. The judge was having none of it, and told her that if what she said was true, then she had to hope for justice from a higher tribunal. He told her:

'I fear that in addition to this poor child, others have become the victims of your cruel inhumanity. Of those poor children, four in number, at least three have been put to death by you and those by whom you were assisted. It is necessary that the strong arm of the law should vindicate the justice of the country, and take up the cause of these poor helpless and innocent children'.

When her sister Sarah was brought back for her sentencing, the judge told her that the sentence on Margaret Waters should instill in her the need for remorse for the deeds she had committed. He then ordered that she be imprisoned for 18 calendar months with hard labour.

Margaret Waters was taken to Horsemonger Lane Gaol in a cab escorted by two warders from Newgate prison, and it was reported that once there, the firmness with which she had exhibited throughout the trial disappeared. Before she had left for the prison, she had a meeting with her sister and both women were extremely upset, although Waters continued to assert that she never meant to kill any of the children. It was then announced that the date of her execution was to be Tuesday 11 October and there were many discussions in the national newspapers as to whether her sentenced would be commuted. Some people thought that the death sentence, would hopefully send a message to deter other women thinking about taking up baby farming as a profession. One newspaper stated that 'there is unfortunately an acknowledgement in what passes for the public mind, that the life of an infant is lesser than that of an adult'. In view of the strong feelings regarding hanging a woman, the consensus was very much that Waters would get off. It was reported that although she continued to maintain her innocence, she had difficulty in accounting for the large amount of money found on her when she was arrested. It also indicated that she could well afford to feed well and clothe all the children that she had supposedly 'adopted'.

Most of the newspapers condemned the whole trade of baby farming, once again alleging that some of the blame had to be laid at the feet of many proprietors of newspapers containing the adverts which baby farmers used. Others tried to apportion blame elsewhere. Following the Waters' trial one paper blamed:

'A newspaper clerk who received 27 advertisements from the same individuals, though with different names, ought to have excited some suspicion, which should have led to his counseling his principals upon the subject. In such a case, a simple enquiry might have been made and the disgusting trade checked, if not put an end to. After what has taken place there can be no excuse for negligence in the future, and we trust that a rule will be adopted in every newspaper office, that no advertisement for the adoption or nursing of children shall be allowed to appear'.

It seems that Water's two brothers who had visited their sister in prison, had approached Lord Chief Baron and informed him that they had evidence that their sister had treated one of the children, of whose murder she had been convicted, with great kindness. The judge told them that evidence of that kind would have been important if it had been produced at the trial, but it was not within his remit to do anything about it now and therefore the law must take its course. The brothers then forwarded the same information to the Home Secretary, but he too decided not to interfere

Once Margaret Water received the sentence of death, she naturally became very despondent and refused to eat and the prison staff were forced to administer stimulants to encourage her. The Chaplain, Mr Jessop urged her to confess and on the day before her execution she was asked to write out her confession. In the statement she described the financial worries that had led her to getting into baby farming, and admitted that she had been guilty of obtaining money through false pretences. In the confession she said that if she had not given the children proper food, it was an error of judgment and declared that she had never given the children food that was sour. Again she declared herself innocent of the deaths of the children in the workhouse, and claimed that she had been convicted of the death of baby Cohen, who she had not seen for a fortnight before his death. She too blamed the parents of the children saying that:

'she considered the parents of illegitimate children who wanted to get rid of them by any means, were more to blame than persons like herself. If there were no parents of this class there would be no baby farmers'.

Once again she asserted that she never intended the children to die.

On the morning of her execution, the Chaplain went to her cell at 7 am and they joined in prayer until the hangman Calcraft was introduced. Shortly before 9 am the prison bell began to toll, and Waters was pinioned by the hangman before being taken into the little prison yard where the scaffold had been erected. The procession was headed by the prison governor, Mr John Keene and he was followed by Mr Abbot the under-sheriff. They were followed by Waters with the Chaplain at her side, reading from the Burial Service. It was stated that she showed no fear, but rather became very resolute and walked with a firm step towards the scaffold. As soon as the hood was put over her head and the noose adjusted, it was reported that she 'uttered by those who heard it as a beautiful extempore prayer', After shaking hands with Mr Jessop, one of the warders and Mr Calcraft, the bolt was pulled, and one of the most infamous woman of the time ended her life at the end of a rope. It was somewhat ironic that on the very day of her execution two more dead infants were found in Hyde Park.

The execution of Margaret Waters and the abhorrence of the publicity it received, shocked Victorian society. No longer could the problems of infanticide be ignored or swept under the carpet. Indeed it frightened Amelia Dyer to such an extent that she abandoned her career as baby farmer, and went into hiding as an attendant in a lunatic asylum. The last place where the police authorities would have found her.

Chapter Six: Susan King

The next woman was not only a baby farmer, but she was a person who was constantly drunk and aggressive and feared by all her neighbours. This fear of confronting her ensured that her occupation was kept in the dark, and for many months was not reported to the police. Was her constant drinking a way of escaping from the degradation of ill treating the child placed in her care? Thankfully the ill treatment was finally brought to the attention of the authorities by a neighbour, but the case still throws up more questions than answers. Why did the mother, who undoubtedly loved her child and visited her on a regular basis, say nothing whilst her daughter deteriorated in front of her face. Could it be that she was so afraid of the woman's temper that she chose to ignore the fact that her child was being badly neglected? Or could it be that she was more afraid of the publicity that would entail, resulting in her losing a good position as housekeeper?

In January of 1871 Annie Butcher was a single pregnant woman who lived in Wellington Road, Islington. When she gave birth to a little girl on 21 March she named her Alice. The baby was born a bit on the small side, but thankfully she was healthy. Butcher looked after the little girl for a fortnight before she was forced to look for a job. She was lucky enough to obtain a post as housekeeper, and she found a 44 year old woman called Susan King who lived on Kingsland Road, Islington, to care for little Alice. Gratefully Butcher informed the woman that she would pay her 6s a week and would provide any clothing that the child needed. The arrangement began and the money was being paid every Monday evening to King, either by Butcher or her sister. She had made the agreement that she would see the child when she paid the money, but more often than not she was told that the child had been taken out by one of King's daughters. Butcher had noticed that the child was not always clean and that she seemed to be very thin about the face, but she kept the information to herself. When Alice had been with the woman for about a month or six weeks, Butcher was sent for and King told that the little girl might die. It seems that she had formed an abscess on her right section of her chest, and another on the bottom of her stomach. The worried mother arrived and she asked to see the abscess, but King had told her that it had burst. Butcher anxiously examined Alice, but found no sign of anything on the child's skin, although there was a large mark on her shoulder. King told her that an abscess had appeared on her shoulder, which she had put on a poultice and it had cleared up nicely. Gratefully Butcher thanked her for her attention and King then asked her for some extra money for the poultice and medicine that she had purchased. Butcher's fears were allayed when she called again and found that Alice was much better, and saw King in the process of feeding her beef tea. Satisfied on this occasion that her daughter was being properly cared for Butcher left, not knowing how much her little daughter was still being abused.

On 16 September 1871 a lodger at the house on Kingsland Road, a woman called Emma Mills who lived under the rooms which Susan King occupied, heard a baby crying in a most pitiful manner. The sound seemed to be coming from a back room at the house, and she went upstairs into the room in which King lived, and found that there was no one at home. Entering cautiously, she found Alice in the back room almost exhausted from crying. Mills noted that the child was filthy and wet, lying on a few dirty rags with only a nightdress on. There was no covers over the child and it appeared to be very cold. Mills lifted the little girl up and carried her out into the back yard of the house to show her to a neighbour called Mrs Watson. However the woman admitted to being frightened of King, and told her to 'take it back and say nothing about it'. Although Mills later admitted that it broke her heart, she did as requested. But she passed the information onto the police, who in turn, reported it to Mr Edwin Leonard Merchan a relieving officer of the workhouse at Islington. He was informed that a child was being neglected at a house on Kingsland Road, and that the woman who cared for her was called Susan King. She was a woman who was well known to the relieving officer, as being someone of very drunken nature and dissolute habits. On Monday 17 September Mr Merchan visited the house at 7 pm and found the child in a cradle in the corner of the room, being looked after by a girl who was aged about 11 or 12 years of age. Alice looked very emaciated and was still in an indescribably filthy state. Excrement was all around the cradle in which she lay, and alongside her was an empty feeding bottle with nothing in it but the remains of some sour milk. The only food in the house was in a broken jug which contained flour and water.

Mr Merchan reported the case to the workhouse medical officer, Dr Andrew David Duckett and the two men decided to return back to the house. When they arrived at 10 pm they found Susan King was there, although she was drunk and half naked. The child was weighed, and although it was said to be six months old, they found it only weighed 5½ lbs. However in the meantime they noted that there was now food in the house, which had not been there previously. The child was quickly removed and placed in the care of a woman called Mrs Jane Wells of Gardener Cottages, Back Road, Islington, where it rallied for a short while. On 13 October little Alice Butcher succumbed to inflammation of the lung, which was directly caused by the neglect and want of nourishment it had suffered at the hands of Susan King. The baby farmer was quickly arrested and placed in the cells charged with the manslaughter of Alice Butcher. Meanwhile Dr Duckett and Mr Merchan called on King's neighbour's and gradually facts began to emerge of the brutish life this baby farmer led. They told the two officers that King was seldom sober and that she was frequently out, leaving her two children aged only 11 and 7, in charge of Alice. As a consequence the little girl was always wet and dirty, and her eyes were constantly gummed up and in need of washing.

An inquest was held on the body of eight month old Alice Butcher at the Caledonian Arms, Islington by Coroner Dr Lankester on Wednesday 19 October 1871. Mrs Wells stated that when she received the child from Dr Duckett she found it to be completely emaciated, to the point that the bones were sticking through the skin. The only covering that the child was wearing was a night dress and some calico wrapped around its loins. The baby was carefully washed and fed, but sadly she told the inquest, despite her care Alice died on 13 October. Annie Butcher gave evidence that the child was hers, and stated that she sometimes saw her when she paid King, however before she died, she had not seen the little girl for three weeks. Each time she visited King, she managed to make an excuse that the child was asleep or out. The anxious mother stated that she had always kept the payments up to date, and that King was paid every single week in advance. She had also supplied her with plenty of clean clothes for her daughter. King challenged her at this point to say that she only had two nightdresses and one flannel blanket to keep the child warm. Annie told her that:

'you had three night dresses, and whenever you asked for fresh clothing they were given to you. I never refused you, nor did I put you off. If you had asked me for more clothes you might have had them'.

Butcher told the court that she had been told that the child had been removed by the Islington workhouse medical office Dr Duckett on 17 September, and placed in the care of a Mrs Wells. She had last seen the child when it was being looked after by Mrs Wells. The inquest was then postponed for a week.

When the inquest had been resumed, Mr Merchan gave evidence of finding the child, but when he stated that King was intoxicated, she hotly denied the fact. He told her:

'I am certain that you were intoxicated, you had a dress around you but nothing under it, in fact I stopped the dress from falling on the floor. You had the child in your arms and a shawl around it. I observed no other clothes which you had taken off. The child had then been washed and there was clean clothing on it, and a lot of food had been purchased in the meantime, as well as corn flour, biscuits and milk'.

He accused her of only buying the food, after hearing of the visit of the relieving officer from her young daughter. King stated that was not true and that she always bought the food on a Monday night after she had been paid. King's two young daughters told the Coroner that they were forced to leave the child on its own sometimes, whilst they raked over rubbish tips in the area, to try to find something to eat. A post mortem was undertaken by Dr Duckett and he said that he had found no marks on the body, but it was very much emaciated and there were excoriations on the thighs and buttocks. These were usually caused when a child had been left in dirty nappies over a long period of time. These were caused due to the acid nature of the urine. On opening the little body he found that all the organs were healthy, except for the left lung which was very inflamed. The brain was slightly congested, and Dr Duckett gave his opinion that the cause of death was from inflammation of the lungs, which he had no doubt was the result of ill treatment and bad nursing. The surgeon confirmed to the Coroner that when he attended to the house with the relieving officer, that Mrs King was drunk and only partly clothed. When asked if she had anything to say on her own behalf, Susan King denied the evidence of the two men and told the inquest that she was a hard working and sober woman. She claimed that she had always done her best to keep the child clean, and had supplied it with plenty of food. The Coroner summed up and the court was cleared, whilst the jury made their deliberations. On their return they recorded a verdict of manslaughter against Susan King.

The case was heard in front of the Islington magistrates on 20 October 1871 and Mrs Wells was the first to give evidence. She produced the blanket which had been wrapped around the child when it was handed over to her, to show the court. Mrs Wells held up the blanket so that the bench could see it was torn and brown with dirt, even though it had been washed and bleached by the witness. She stated that when she received the child it was filthy, and its appearance was 'quite sickening'. A milkman, John Henry Kelly stated that he had delivered milk morning and afternoon at the house of Mrs King, but it was usually one of the daughters that answered the door. He stated that she had a penny worth of milk daily for herself, her two daughters and the child, although she had recently asked him to leave 1½ d worth. Kelly stated that he had seen the prisoner on about two or three occasions, but every time she had been drunk. At this point King interrupted, and said that the milk he left was all for the baby, and that no one else in the house took milk. Kelly told her that when one of her daughter brought the milk jug to the door, she told him that her mother was 'troubled with indigestion and the doctor had advised her to have rum and milk in the morning'. She confided to the milkman that 'when she puts the rum in, it used to fizz up'. The milkman said that he had seen the baby only a few times, but each time it was with the two girls and that:

'I had seen it before, but the last time I could not help noticing it, the sight of it was enough to make you sick. It was in a filthy state and it did not seem to have a bed gown on, the face was all begrimed with dirt, and it was nothing but skin and bone'.

Dr Duckett stated that when he accompanied Mr Merchan to the house on 17 September they found the prisoner in a very excitable state. They had to knock several times on the door before they gained admittance, and when she did finally open the door the prisoner complained that she had just been going to bed. He described to the magistrates how he had examined little Alice, listened to its lungs with his stethoscope and looked at its tongue. He found the child badly nourished, and that was the reason that it had been removed from the prisoners care. Susan King was found guilty of neglecting Alice Butcher, a child left in her care and was informed that she would take her trial at the Central Criminal Court.

Susan King was tried at the Old Bailey on Wednesday November 22 1871 in front of judge Mr Justice Keating, charged with feloniously killing and slaying Alice Butcher. Mr Lilley conducted the prosecution. Mrs Jane Wells gave evidence of the way in which she had looked after the child, after it had been left with her by Dr Duckett. She reported that she knew the child was being starved and neglected, and had told Annie Butcher so four months previously. King interrupted and said that she had always given the baby 'as much as it could eat', and she blamed Mrs Wells for saying such things to spite her. She told the court that Mrs Wells had only wanted to look after the child herself, when she knew how much Annie Butcher was paying her each week. A neighbour Eleanor Watson gave evidence that she had lived next door to the prisoner for eight or nine months. She saw the child when it had first been given to her neighbour, and at that time it was a fine healthy baby. Afterwards she saw the child frequently in the company of the two children belonging to King, and noted then that it looked very neglected. Mrs Watson stated that the prisoner was a very abusive woman, particularly when she was drunk. She had only once tried to say to her that the child had looked neglected, and was violently abused for saying so. At that point the prisoner shouted out across the courtroom 'Did you ever see me intoxicated' the witness answered 'yes, I never hardly saw you otherwise', to which their was laughter in the court. Emma Mills, the lodger stated that she lived in the same house as the prisoner, and had been there for seven months. The child was already there when she moved in, but she quickly noticed how it was neglected and dirty. Mills said that the child was left in the charge of the two girls, who left it alone in the house, and that as a consequence it used to cry a lot.

On Saturday 16 September the baby had cried so much that 'she felt that she could not bear it any longer' and the lodger went to the room about 9 am and described what she had found. She told the jury that she too had mentioned to King that the child was badly neglected, and that she had been abused by the drunken woman. One of the jury asked her if she knew the child's mother, and asked her why she did not mention to her the concerns about the child. Mills answered that two women regularly came to pay King on a Monday night, and the prisoner had told her that one was the mother and the other the aunt. Consequently she did not know which one was the mother. Shortly before the relieving officer came to the house, she had threatened Mrs King that she would tell the mother about the state of the child, but after that the child had been removed and she never saw the two women again. At this point in the trial the prisoner was asked if she had anything to say in her defence and King told the judge 'I am not guilty. I have no witnesses, because no one knows anything about my affairs. I do not make myself sociable with anybody'. Mr Justice Keating summed up for the jury and Susan King was found guilty. The judge told the prisoner that:

'you have been convicted upon the clearest possible evidence of having most shamefully neglected this unfortunate child. It is well that all persons should know that nurses who undertake the care of children, are bound by law to take reasonable and proper care of them, and that culpable neglect of that duty exposed them to be criminally prosecuted. I have to say that this is a particularly bad case, because you have persistently ill treated the child, and that it was utterly neglected and left in a state that was perfectly horrible to think of'

He concluded that he accepted that the neglect was caused by her constant drunkenness but that 'could not be admitted as an excuse in a court of justice'. He then sentenced Susan King to eighteen months imprisonment with hard labour. Many people felt that this sentence was far too light, for the persistent and terrible way in which poor Alice Butcher had suffered at the hands of Susan King.

Chapter Seven: Betsy Binmore

In an attempt to put an end to the increasing numbers of baby farmers, the Government introduced the Infant Life Protection Act in 1872. This made the registration of persons who looked after two or more children under one year of age, compulsory. They would now be issued with a certificate and regular inspections would be held. The authorities hoped that by these women having to be registered, any deaths that took place in the house would have to be notified and brought to the attention of the police. The Government hoped that this would put an end to the multiple deaths which were taking place in the houses of these monsters. However the case of Betsy Binmore illustrated the way in which the Act failed, in that there was no clarity on who should enforce it. Many thought it was the responsibility of the workhouse relieving officers or police officers to visit and inspect the premises. After a while the Government appointed Inspectors from the Board of Health, but they soon asked to be relieved of this responsibility as the cost of employing Inspectors was seen to be yet another drain on, already overstretched local budgets. Most people just chose to ignore it. On May 1873 it was reported that in the whole of London alone, in the short time the Act had been in force, only twenty five certificates had been issued. This case also indicated the unwilling way in which doctors of the period would visit poor people and their families.

Betsy Binmore lived at Wolborough Court near Newton Abbot, Devon in March of 1875 where she had lived for the past twelve months. It was not known when she began her career as a baby farmer, but by the second week of August 1874 this 43 year old former char woman, agreed to look after a little girl called Margaret Phillips. The child was as usual illegitimate, and her mother was Mary Phillips who gave birth to the child in the workhouse at Newton Abbott on 1 August. She was a fine, full grown, healthy child and the pair remained in the workhouse for a further two weeks after her birth. Whilst there, little Margaret was fed on bread and milk and had one pint of milk a day, consisting of half a pint in the morning and another half pint in the evening. Margaret was at first looked after by a woman called Mrs Hall, where she stayed for a week, and then Mary Phillips left the workhouse and went to stay at Betsy Binmore's house. She was there for a fortnight when she managed to get a job in Torquay, and Binmore agreed to nurse little Margaret for 2s 6d a week. The two women arranged that Mary Phillips would pay 10s at the end of each month for the keep of the child. The situation worked out well and the mother saw the child regularly, but on 2 November she obtained a post in service at Bath. The night before she started work, Mary Phillips kept the child with her, and it was then a healthy three month old little girl who, as it was reported at the time, 'ate its meat freely'. It was also agreed that Binmore would send her mother a letter every week reporting on how the child was progressing.

A week before Christmas, Binmore asked her daughter to go to Dr Nathaniel Haydon at Newton Abbott and ask him to come and see one of the children that she looked after, who was ill. She had by now another two children in the house as well as a child of her own and she was helped out by her daughter Sarah Jane. Dr Haydon asked the girl if she had a certificate from the workhouse for him to attend to the child. She told him that it was not a parish case and that her mother would pay him. The doctor told her he was very busy and would not be able to get there before 8 pm that night. When he arrived in the evening, Dr Haydon appeared to be more concerned over who was going to pay him, rather than attending to his patient. When Binmore explained that she would get the money from the child's mother, he told her that he would not attend until he was paid and he left. Binmore then asked her daughter to go to fetch another doctor who was called Dr Jayne, but he too declined to attend when he learned that her mother did not have a certificate from the relieving officer. Just before Christmas of 1874 a neighbour, Ann Mudge who also lived in Wolborough Court was asked to go to Binmore's house. She noted that the little girl named Margaret had looked ill and wasted, and she urged her neighbour to call in a doctor. She also commented that the other children looked ill too. Mudge had thought the children were not being fed properly, as she had seen Binmore feed the baby on boiled bread. On 4 January 1875 she saw Dinmore with the little girl Margaret on her knee, and the child looked like it was dying. She remonstrated with her for not bringing in a doctor, and Binmore told her that she could not get a doctor to attend. Needless to say little Margaret Phillips died later that day, and her death threw Binmore into a panic. The next day she went to the house of Police Sergeant Nicholls and she told him that she was in trouble. Binmore said that one of the children she looked after was dead, and that although she had asked three doctors to attend, none of them would come to see the child. Binmore told the sergeant that she had also been to the house of the relieving officer three times in order to get a certificate from him for a doctor to attend, but he was never at home.

The sergeant went to the Registrar of Births and Deaths but he would not give him a death certificate until the Coroner had been informed. An inquest was arranged and, as was usual at that time, when the jury went to the house to see the little girls body, they were amazed to find two other small children there, in an equally perilous state of health. They were both emaciated and appeared to be too weak to cry. Susan Bartlett, a nurse from Newton Abbott workhouse was sent to see the children, and she barely recognised the body of little Margaret Phillips. She had known the deceased child from her birth and could barely recognised her as she was so shriveled and emaciated. When Margaret had been born she had been a fine, healthy child. The nurse saw the condition of the two other unnamed children, who were also very thin and she had them removed immediately to the workhouse hospital. One was a boy of 5 months who weighed only 7 lbs and a few ounces, and he also had been born in the union workhouse. The other child was a little girl who weighed just 4 ozs more.

At the inquest Dr Gay gave evidence that he had been called to examine the body of the child, Margaret Phillips at the prisoners house by the Coroner. He found the child excessively thin, the skin was wrinkled and all roundness and plumpness was gone. He could find no indication of disease to account for the emaciation. When the prisoner asked him what was the cause of death, he told Binmore harshly that she had starved the child. After the body had been removed, he had undertaken a post mortem and found a marked absence of any fatty matter. The stomach was distended, but the intestines were collapsed and empty, and there was only a small amount of fluid in the stomach. There was no trace of disease and the brain of the child was normal. He told the Coroner that he attributed the death to 'the entire want of nourishment'. The next day he had seen the two other children who had been removed to the workhouse, and found their bones protruding and the skin wrinkled. The jury brought in a verdict of manslaughter and Betsy Binmore was taken into custody by the Coroners order to take her trial at the next Devon Assizes.

On Saturday 13 March 1875 the case was discussed by the judge Sir Robert Lush at the Devon Lent Assizes, who told the Grand Jury that it was case of a very serious nature in which the woman had been charged with the murder of an infant. He described the circumstances of the case, and that she had been found guilty of murder, but the Coroner's jury had only found her guilty of manslaughter. He compared it to 'a case similar to one that occurred in the same neighbourhood some years ago, which was a reference to Charlotte Winsor. He told the Grand Jury that in that particular case a woman had received a lump sum to adopt the child, and therefore had a direct interest in putting it out of its existence. But in this instance it was in the woman's own interests to keep the child alive as she was being paid money to care for it. He described the amount of milk that had been delivered to the house was quite insufficient for the number of children she was caring for. He warned the jury that they must be very clear in their own minds that the woman had deliberately starved the children in order to make as much as she could. Three days later Betsy Binmore appeared before Mr Justice Lush at the assizes which were held at Exeter Castle. When she appeared she was undefended, but the judge asked one of the court, Mr Bompas to defend the prisoner.

The first witness was the mother of the child Mary Phillips, and she told the judge that at the workhouse she had fed the child on plenty of milk and bread. She did not know how much milk the child had whilst she was with Mrs Binmore, but thought it was fed on milk and cornflour. She admitted receiving letters every week from the prisoner, but as she did not wish her employers to know that she had given birth to an illegitimate child, the letters had been burned. When she was cross examined she did admit that the child did not like being fed from the bottle. Susan Bartlett, the nurse at the Newton Abbot workhouse told the judge that the child was a fine, baby when it was born and had not been ill whilst she was at the workhouse. She had not seen the child until it was dead, and had barely recognised it. She told the court that the 5 month old boy that had been removed from Binmore's house, now weighed 11 lbs after being cared for at the workhouse. The boy too had been born in the union workhouse and once again she said it was a fine little child when he was born. The little girl had also improved though she weighed less than the boy.

Mary Hall told the court that she was the wife of William Hall and they lived at Newton Abbott and she had nine children of her own. She too confirmed that she had the child for a week before it was removed by the mother, and given to the prisoner to nurse. It was a small child, but when she heard that it was dead, had gone to the workhouse to see the body. Mrs Hall too told the judge that she barely recognised it as the one she had looked after for so short a time. Neighbour Ann Mudge stated that the prisoner always appeared to be fond of the children, and they were all kept fairly clean. Sarah Jane Binmore then gave evidence that her mother took in children to nurse, and she remember Mary Phillips coming to the house and living there for a fortnight before she went to work at Torquay. She agreed to pay 2s 6d a week for the baby and she thought that her mother earned as much again from the other children. She also drew 1s 6d from the parish workhouse, and that was all she had to live on. Sarah Jane told the judge that she did not earn anything herself while she was at her mother's house, but she helped out with the children. The girl said that a milkman called Mr Webber used to deliver milk daily. She could not remember exactly how much they had delivered, but she remembered that they had both scald and raw milk. (Scald was milk that had been boiled to rid it of impurities, whereas raw milk was untouched and fresh from the cow). She thought they had a quart of scald milk for a penny and a pennyworth of raw milk delivered every day, and sometime the babies had cornflour and milk. Ominously the girl then told the judge that they had lived in Fore Court before they moved to Wolborough Court, and that three babies had died there before Margaret Phillips death. She claimed however that they had all been attended by a doctor before they died. When cross examined, she stated that she thought the doctors had been Dr Drake and Dr Haydon. Sarah Jane said that the children were very well fed by her mother, and they had bread and sugar as well as cornflour and milk. They were fed three or four times a day and always had a bottle of milk at night. Sarah Webber the wife of the milkman said that up to Christmas they supplied the prisoner with milk. They had one penny worth of milk in the morning and a half penny at night if she could get it. Her husband corroborated his wife's evidence.

Chemist Mr James Ponsford told the jury that Mrs Binmore had brought a child in for him to look at the week before Christmas, and he noted that it was thin and weak. He gave the woman some powders which he said would build the child up a little, He thought that the child was suffering from acidity of the stomach. Dr Haydon then took the stand and he stated that he had been a practicing surgeon for many years in Newton Abbott, and was also a medical officer for the workhouse. He had known the prisoner for about two years and had attended her house to see a child in July 1873. The child was only six months old and he had attended to it just once. Dr Haydon told the court that he thought it was suffering from a wasting disease, and therefore was not surprised when he heard that the child was dead. The judge asked him to clarify what the definition of a wasting disease was. The surgeon told him that wasting could be seen occasionally in even the best cared for children, and that it was caused by insufficient or improper food. He said that anything but milk food is very likely to disagree with children brought up by hand. He believed that among poor families, a large proportion of children not having breast milk died in infancy. Cross examined he agreed that the child he had attended might have been suffering from want of proper food. He described the girl Sarah Jane coming to his surgery and he told her that he must be paid, as he had called at the house to see sick children three times before and never got paid. When Mrs Binmore told him she had no money, he told her to get a certificate from the workhouse before he went away. He told the judge that the relieving officer lived no more than five minutes away from the prisoner's house, and she could have easily got a certificate from him. The next day was Board Day at the Newton Abbott workhouse and that was when he heard of the death of the child. Dr Haydon said that afterwards he had seen the two other children which had been brought from the prisoners house, and he thought they were all suffering from the want of proper food. With care and attention the two children had both recovered. He gave his opinion that two quarts of scald milk would not be sufficient for three children. A child of three or four months would require a pint and a half of new milk per day, and would require more as it grew older, unless other food was added.

Dr Drake, also of Newton Abbott, told the judge that he too knew the prisoner and that during the year of 1873 he had been called out twice by her to attend to two children, both of which had died. Both had been very much emaciated and one was only three weeks old and the other four months. Atrophy or infantile consumption had been the cause of death of one of the children. He stated that it might have been caused by insufficient food, but it was his opinion that the atrophy was the cause of death. On January 4 the prisoner had requested him to go to her house, and he refused because he had not been paid for his last visit. Another surgeon Dr Jayne described for the court how he too had been called out to the prisoners house, and he also had declined to go for the same reason. Dr Gay gave his findings from the post mortem, and explained to the court that the poor often brought up their children with bread to thicken the milk they gave to a child. Mr Elias Ford, one of the members of the Board of Guardians for the workhouse next gave evidence. He stated that he had met the prisoner on January 4 and she told him that she had a baby at home poorly. She said that the baby had ruptured a blood vessel the week before, and she had applied to two medical men, but they would not attend. Mr Ford asked her if she had more babies at home, and she told him that she had. He told her to get a certificate from the relieving officer, and she went away, walking in the direction of the man's house.

William Roberts said that he was the assistant relieving officer at Newton Abbott and he had been at home on the day the prisoner's child had died, but she never made any application to him that day, or at any time during the previous week. James Snelling Beard said that he was the Registrar of Deaths for Newton Abbot and prior to 5 January, four children had died at the prisoners house since July 1873. Binmore's defence counsel, Mr Bompas then rose to defend the prisoner. He called as a witness another neighbour Mary Waycott, who told the court she had known the prisoner for three years, and during that time had always found her kind hearted to the children in her care. Mr Bompas maintained that there was not a shred of evidence that the prisoner had any intention of killing any of the children. He claimed that the prisoner's offence, was one of omission rather than anything else. One piece of evidence that he thought was conclusive of her case, was the fact that it was in her own interests that she kept all the children alive, because she was receiving 2s 6d a week each for their upkeep. It might be in her interest to keep the children on as little food as she could, to make a small profit out of the half crown each she was paid, but it was evident that it was not in her interest to destroy them. The judge told the jury that they must satisfy themselves before they could find the prisoner guilty of the capital charge of murder. They must be sure that the child was starved to death and that the prisoner in doing so, intended to destroy its life. If on the other hand they were of the opinion that she had failed in her duty, through her desire to keep the child on as little as possible, they must only find her guilty of the lesser crime of manslaughter.

The jury after a short deliberation found Betsy Binmore guilty of manslaughter. The judge in passing sentence said that in his opinion, the verdict of the jury was the only one at which they could arrive on the evidence before them. He thanked Mr Bompas for his great ability and stated that 'I cannot allow the opportunity to pass without thanking the learned counsel, who at my own request had undertaken this defence and had bestowed upon it so much effort'. Turning to the prisoner in the dock he told her:

'I commiserate with you very much in your position, but I feel a public example in this case must be made by passing on you a heavy sentence. Baby farming has been practiced to a large extent in this country in violation of the present laws. It is necessary to make an example in order that persons, who undertake the care of young children might know what the law requires of them. Therefore as a warning to others, I feel that I could not impose a less sentence than penal servitude for a considerable term, and that term will be twelve years'.

The prisoner was removed from the dock crying bitterly. On Monday 22 March 1874 the matter was brought up in the House of Commons by MP Mr Charley who questioned the Home Secretary, Mr Cross as to why Betsy Binmore had not been registered for caring for the children under the Infant Life Protection Act. He told the house that three or four other infants which had been entrusted to her care had died, and he called upon the Home Secretary to issue a circular to the local authorities calling their attention to the Act and requiring them to enforce it. Mr Cross replied that the judge himself, Mr Justice Lush had also informed him that the case had been a 'bad one' and he too had queried why Mrs Binmore had not been registered. Mr Charley stated that he would ask for a list of all registered baby farmer the following day. Questions were also asked at the Board of Guardians meeting at Newton Abbot on Wednesday 24 March when a letter had been received from the Grand Jury asking why the relieving officer had failed to call at the house. The relieving officer stated that he had not visited, as he was not aware that the woman had any children under her care. On the few occasions he had visited, there had not been any children at the house. It was agreed that the workhouse clerk would draw up a reply to that effect.

Chapter Eight: Sophia Martha Todd and Mary Dennis

Most of the baby farmers in this book were poor ignorant women with no skills to speak of and little formal education, but there were exceptions. Sophia Martha Todd saw herself as a woman who did not conform to this rule. She had been a teacher and a governess, and never for one minute would she have pictured herself standing in a dock convicted of baby farming. Todd used her education in order to write charming and persuasive letters to young pregnant girls offering them a better kind of live for their babies. Yet like many other women who took up this sordid profession, she callously 'adopted' children, before disposing of them in a manner which can only be surmised. There is no doubt that she hoped that by giving herself airs and graces, that she was able to command a better premium for the children that she took in. Labelled 'the Lancashire Governess' she only escaped the noose it was thought, because she was educated, and had the confidence to display a more gentle bearing than some of her more unfortunate sisters.

Sophia Martha Todd was aged 35 and from the beginning of the case was described as being 'ladylike in her appearance'. She had certainly led a more refined upbringing than many of the other women in this book. Her father was a civil engineer named Wilson who came from Glasgow who, according to his daughter had moved amongst the 'best society of that city'. A few years later Mr Wilson moved to Barbados where he married his second wife, a West Indian lady, the daughter of a wealthy planter. The couple had Sophia, who was born on the Isle of Wight, but sadly her mother died when she was only a child, and as a consequence Mr Wilson returned back to England alone with his daughter. He was determined that she would received a good education, and he sent her to Brussels to one of the finest schools of the period. After leaving school however, Wilson found himself in somewhat reduced circumstances, and as a result his daughter had to take on the role of governess to several respectable families in Brussels. It was while Miss Wilson was there that she was offered a job in Russia, teaching in an old Polish nobleman's family, where she quickly became fluent in both in Polish and Russian. She returned to England and was for a while living with relatives in Yorkshire, and whilst there she got a post caring for the children of the Earl of Ducie at Bowness in Windermere. Miss Wilson later claimed that during that time she was employed as a teacher and a daily governess to four 'of the best families in Bowness'. It was said that she was thoroughly accomplished in the fine arts and could speak five different languages.

Some years later she taught music and languages at Lancaster and at that place had met a man called Mr Thomas Jackson, a small farmer who she married in St Luke's Church, Hardman Street, Liverpool. Unfortunately Jackson was soon reduced to giving up his farm, and he got a post working on the railway at Ulverstone. The marriage failed and within a few months his wife had moved out of the marital home and into another address on Prescott Street, Liverpool. Ever resourceful, she quickly found employment at the Victoria Hotel, Liverpool as a book keeper. It was estimated that around this time she learned of the death of her former husband. Despite being employed as a book keeper Mrs Jackson, as she was then, decided that she could make more money looking after children. It was reported at the time of her trial that 'no reason was ever given, as to why she fell from respectable employment into that despised profession'. Like many others before her and in order to hide her crime, she changed her name several times when she advertised for babies to adopt. But there was no ambiguity about the cost, as in her replies she clearly stated that 'a premium was expected'. Only when a reply came to the anonymous newspaper box-office number which she used, would she give a name and address, which was usually false. About this time she also formed a relationship with a man called Todd, who was then an agent for Day's Menagerie and she lived with him as his wife in Liverpool and later in Wavertree.

Her husband then obtained a position as agent for Fawcett's Circus and the couple moved to Manchester. The next time his wife emerged it was around 1875 when she was back in Liverpool once more. She was lodging at the house of a Miss Mary Jane Joliffe in Prospect Street, Liverpool and she had an infant with her. Todd told her landlady that it was the child of a Dr and Mrs George, and she was caring for it whilst they attended a party. She said that they would be calling for the child on their return from the party, so Miss Joliffe was not surprised to see her without the child the next day. Todd then went to live at another lodging house belonging to a Mrs Mary Ann Oldham where she called herself Mrs Jackson. When she moved out ten days later, without paying her rent, she foolishly left a box behind. Todd later wrote a letter to Mrs Oldham dated 17 January 1876. The letter read:

'My dear Mrs Oldham - I have just arrived from London after being there for several weeks settling some important business: now that it is finished, and I shall be at liberty to settle with you and bring my box away. I am sure you must have thought me most neglectful, but having now settled my affairs you will not find yourself a loser. You may expect me to pay you a visit any day between this and Saturday -
Yours truly U E JACKSON'

Despite her promise, Todd never went back to pay her dues and six months later when the box was finally opened by Mrs Oldham, she was horrified to find in it the mummified body of a baby. Rags had surrounded the body, which had effectively eliminated any smell from decomposition. The police were called in, and enquiries were made and a description of Sophia Todd was given, which was circulated to other police forces. As a result she was found at the Old Trafford, near Manchester in a trap with the man who she claimed was her husband. Sophia Todd was immediately arrested on a charge of murder and taken to Devon Street Police Station, Manchester where she made a comprehensive statement. When she was asked who the dead child was, she told the police an unlikely story. She claimed that one day she had been visited by a fair haired man called Mr Lord. He told her that he had been sent by the putative father of a child, in order for it to be adopted. He asked her to take the child, as yet unborn, and he offered a premium of £10. Todd agreed and about five weeks later the child was delivered to her by a woman, who was accompanied by the young man called Lord. She said that he had brought with him the agreed sum of money. He told her that he would come to her house again the next morning at 8.30 am to give an address, where she could communicate with the father of the child, who was most anxious not to lose touch with his baby. Todd told the police however that about 3.30 am the next morning, as she was trying to feed the child 'it just stretched itself out. I held it close to me and it stretched out again and died'.

Unbelievably Todd told the Station Superintendent that she did not know if the child was a boy or a girl apart from a comment she said that the lady had said to her 'hoping that she would be lucky with my little son'. She then described how, when the child was dead, she placed it in the box. Todd stated that she was very afraid that she would be found out the following morning when the young man appeared at her door. However Todd concluded her statement by telling the Superintendent that she never saw the man calling himself Mr Lord again. When she arrived the police station at Devon Street she was searched, and in her possession was found a letter from a Mr Henry Thompson. He was offering £10 as a premium for her to keep another child. The letter was addressed to Box No K57 of the *Liverpool Mercury* office and was dated 29 March 1875. The letter read as follows:

'Mrs Jackson - In reply to yours of the 15th and judging from the kindly tone of your letter. I will be very glad for you to take the babe, but it will not be born before the middle of July. The reason I wish to arrange so early is that I have to go abroad, and will not be back until August. The child will entirely be given up to you. The parents are young and healthy. I could only give you £10 with it. Answer at once and oblige Yours truly HENRY THOMPSON'

There was also another letter from someone called John Robinson, asking for details of her terms and offering to pay £30 premium for a child to be adopted.

Sophia Todd was brought before the Liverpool stipendiary magistrate, Mr Raffles on Monday March 26 1877 on suspicion of causing the murder of an unnamed child. She appeared at the court looking very fashionably dressed, but despite her beautiful clothes she was undefended. When Mr Raffles questioned why she did not have a solicitor, she told him that the man Todd had deserted her once she had been apprehended, and that she had no friends to help her. The prosecuting solicitor, Mr Davies stated that she was charged on suspicion of causing the death of a male child, who seemed from his remains to be only a few months old. He stated that for the past few years she had been carrying on the business of baby farming, and he produced the two letters as evidence. Miss Mary Jane Joliffe the landlady of the lodging house in Prospect Street, Liverpool gave evidence that she had seen the child with Todd in the summer of 1875. Miss Joliffe had sat with the prisoner until 2 am, as she was still waiting for the doctor and his wife to return, but feeling tired she left Todd and went to her own bed. The next morning the prisoner had stated that the doctor and his wife had picked up the baby soon after Miss Joliffe had retired for the night. She gave her landlady the reason for the late appearance of the doctor and his wife was because Mrs George had been taken ill, and 'it had been difficult to find some brandy'. Miss Joliffe told the court that when she last saw the baby, it had been wrapped in a very distinctive shawl, which was red with a black border and she later saw her lodger wearing that very same shawl. Miss Joliffe told the magistrates that in November of 1875 the prisoner left her lodgings, still owing rent and went to those belonging to Mrs Oldham of Springfield Street, Liverpool. She said that her lodger had left the box at her house, and after a while a cab arrived and the box was loaded onto it and taken away to her new lodgings.

The next witness was the landlady, Mrs Oldham who told the court that Todd only stayed at her house for ten days or more, before she departed, once again owing the rent. After she had gone, Mrs Oldham found she had left some belongings behind, including the box. She explained how she was forced to place an advertisement in the local newspaper stating that unless the owner removed the box, the contents and the box would be sold to pay off the rent that was still outstanding. No one came to claim the box which was then opened and the discovery of the dead child was found. She told the magistrate that the box had been securely locked and no perceptible smell was emanating from it. Dr Cormack took the stand and said that he had made a close medical examination of mummified remains of the body. He stated that the child was a little boy and that it had died when its head had been crushed. He estimated that the body had been in the box for a year, as its skin had taken on a leathery appearance. There was much discussion on a wrinkle of skin around the neck which looked like it could have been a cut throat, but Dr Cormack gave his opinion that it was unlikely that the child had died in this manner. During the medical evidence it was reported that the prisoner had showed some signs of emotion. The magistrate, Mr Raffles asked Todd if she had any statement to make, and she said that she had nothing further to add, and was remanded for a week. Police enquiries established that Todd had obtained at least six children by inserting advertisements for adoption, when various premiums had being paid. However none of these children had ever been seen alive again.

On Saturday April 14 1877 Todd was once more brought up before Mr Raffles, and the first witness was Dr J Campbell Brown the borough analyst who had undertaken the post mortem on the remains. He reported his findings to the court and said that the little boy had been full grown, well developed and had not died from natural causes, however because of the mummification he could not suggest how it had died. He had surmised that it might have been poisoned and he examined the contents of the stomach, but no arsenic had been found. Todd, who had sat throughout the examination with her head in her hands, was asked if she had anything to say, but she simply shook her head. Mr Raffles informed her that he was sentencing her to take her trial at the next assizes. Sophia Martha Todd was brought in front of Mr Justice Henry Hawkins at the Liverpool Assizes on Friday 26 September 1877. Mr Potter and Mr Lewis Williams were for the prosecution and thankfully by now Todd was defended by a Mr Cummings. When she was brought into the court, she again hid her face in her hands and appeared to be crying. Mr Justice Hawkins ordered that she was given a chair to sit in for the duration of the proceedings, which lasted from 10 am to 7 pm. Her defence counsel, Mr Cummings stated that in his opinion there was no certainty as to the injury to the child found in the box, and therefore the case relied on circumstantial evidence at the very least. He told the jury that because of the lack of evidence against the prisoner, he was confident that she would be acquitted. The judge summed up the case for the jury and commented on the letter from Mr Henry Thompson offering a premium for her to adopt the child. He told them that:

'a strange mode of life was exhibited in the correspondence, that a woman should take the absolute charge of the child of people who were perfect strangers to her, and keep

and nourish it in the way a little child should be kept for, what appeared to be, the miserable sum of £10'.

The jury retired to consider their verdict and appeared a mere forty minutes later. They found Todd guilty of wilful murder. The judge told her:

'I can come to no other conclusion, other than that upon that night in July when this poor innocent baby was brought to you, it was brought for its destruction, and ere the morning sun dawned, you had barbarously murdered it'.

He then assumed the black cap and passed on her the sentence of death. Todd was then removed and taken to Kirkdale Gaol, where it was reported that she spent most of her time crying, but whether she cried for the children she had murdered, or for herself was never truly established. On August 3 1877 there was an announcement that a reprieve was being sought for the prisoner by her defence counsel, Mr Cummings. He had appealed to the Home Secretary Rt. Hon. Richard Asheton Cross MP for the decision of the jury to be overturned. Mr Cummings made several points in his petition claiming that Todd had never tried to conceal the fact that she had advertised to adopt a child, which unfortunately had died on the same night. He dismissed the medical evidence and stated that when the remains of the child had been examined, there were no external wounds on the body. Therefore Mr Cummings claimed that the child had died, as the prisoner had stated, of convulsions. He deplored the fact that the jury had formed the impression that she had intentionally murdered the child. Lastly he pointed out that she had made no serious attempts to conceal the body, and if she had been truly guilty of murder, she would have taken more care to conceal the box in which the body lay for months undetected. It seems that a lot of people agreed with him. Later it was said that over 2,000 signatures had been signed. At the same time it was also announced that Todd had not been visited by a single friend or relative during her incarceration, and the only visits she received was from Mr Piggott the Prison Chaplain.

On Thursday 9 August 1877 it was announced that Todd was to be executed on Monday 13 August, despite the petition. On Saturday 11 August, Dr Cormack and Justice Hawkins were summoned to London, and following a meeting with the Home Secretary, a telegram was delivered to the gaol stating that a reprieve had been granted. This was later followed by a formal notification. When the news was given to Todd by the governor, Major Leggett and the Chaplain Mr Piggott, she burst into hysterical weeping. Following this reprieve it was reported that 'the prisoner remained resigned and accepting of her fate'. The case provided much discussion in the local and national newspapers, where opinions seemed divided. Many people simply thought Todd was innocent because of her demure and ladylike appearance. Only after her reprieve, was it established that whilst living on Prescott Street, Liverpool she obtained a child from Whitehaven to adopt, which she took out one day and was never seen again. About five other children had been seen with her on different occasions and when questioned about them she said that had all died natural deaths. Another child she had adopted was found mysteriously suffocated in bed, and in that instance the inquest jury returned a verdict of 'found suffocated'. This was quite a common occurrence at a time when children shared the same beds as adults. The next child that she adopted was in 1875, and this was the same child with which she had been tried and convicted. Debates about the innocence or guilt of Sophia Martha Todd persisted, long after the sentence was commuted to life imprisonment. This was mainly due to her repeated statement that she was quite innocent, and the medical report of Mr Cummings which alleged that the child might possibly have died of convulsions. Other reports claimed that despite the fact that she was an educated and refined young lady, whilst she lived in Bowness it was known that she had left the area owing money to many of the tradesmen of the area.

The sins of Sophia Martha Todd however pale into insignificance to the crimes of another baby farmer, whose case shocked the newspaper reading public, who were now used to the descriptions of children left in these baby farmers care. It was also one of the few I have read about, where once again the mother seemed to be complicit in the death of her child. The matter only came to light following a meeting of the Truro Board of Guardians on Wednesday 14 November 1877. An unnamed woman made a complaint to Superintendent Angel of the Truro Police, that an eleven month old child was being starved by her neighbour. Together with Mr Richards a relieving officer for the workhouse, the men had visited the address and demanded to see the child. Mary Dennis, aged 58 told him it was upstairs, and that she was waiting for a clergyman to come to baptize it 'for fear anything might happen to it'. There they found the child was a perfect skeleton, the ribs and back being almost fleshless. The condition of the child was so poor, that its lower limbs had mortified. Mr Richards was appalled at what he saw and he returned and asked the medical officer of the workhouse, Mr Sharp to visit the child the next day. Mr Sharp went to the house as requested and he declared that there was no medical reason for the child's condition, apart from absolute neglect and starvation from which it had suffered. They asked Dennis what she had fed the child on, as it was obviously in a starving condition, and she told the two men, bread and water and occasionally milk and sugar. She told them she had done all she could for the child, but the mother only paid her 1s or 1s 2d a week. Mr Sharp wanted to remove it to the workhouse, but because of the weakness of the child, he wanted it to eat first. It was taken to a neighbour's house where it ravenously ate everything that was offered to it. The child was then given to the relieving officer, Mr Richards who took it to the workhouse.

Dennis had defended herself by stating that she had not sufficient money to provide better food for the child, and that he had been a fussy eater and often refused food. The following day the matter was brought before the guardians. The vice-chairman Mr Clyma described the condition of the child and he told his colleagues that he felt that this case was so bad that the Board should take proceedings against this baby farmer, 'what ever the cost might be'. To the normally miserly decisions the board usually took when spending the ratepayers money, this decision was greeted by cheers in the boardroom. Mr Clyma said that the matter had only come to light when Dennis had fallen out with an unnamed neighbour who had complained to the police about the woman's treatment of a child in her care. The child was called William John Bray and its mother had been a married woman named Emily Bray, although the child was illegitimate. Mrs Bray had claimed that her husband had deserted her about three years previously, and she had been forced to find work as a servant, at the Bridge Inn at Truro. It was there that eleven months previously she had given birth to the male child. It was decided by the guardians that 'the clerk take such steps for the prosecution of the woman Dennis as soon as possible'. Superintendent Angel got a warrant and the woman was arrested the following day. Unfortunately before anything more could be done to save the child, it died. Police enquiries established that Mary Dennis also ran a lying-in house, and like many others then made arrangement to take care of the child for a weekly fee. Emily Bray was desperate enough to have left the child in Dennis's care. The baby farmer fed it nothing but bread and water, and as a consequence the child, who had been a healthy eleven months old, was quickly reduced to a skeletal condition.

An inquest was held at the workhouse on Friday 16 November before Coroner Mr John Carlyon. Dr Sharp the workhouse medical officer told the Coroner that the mother paid Dennis 3s 8d a week, out of which only 1s 2d was used for the maintenance of the child. About a month after the birth a medical man, Dr Quicke had been called in, but since that time no one had seen the child for the last four months. Dr Sharp stated that he had first seen the child on 7 November when he arranged for it to be brought to the workhouse the following day. He told the Coroner that he knew from the first that the situation was dire, and did not expect the little boy to live. There were no bruises on the body but the buttocks were very red, which was presumably from being constantly in a wet napkin, and there were many marks of flea bites on the body. When he undertook the post mortem after the child had died, he found inflammation in the liver, kidneys and intestines, which had resulted from the child being fed improper food. The marks of inflammation were of long standing, and might have arisen from exposure to cold. He concluded that the cause of death was the want of proper food and of care. The Coroner told the jury that he had consulted Taylor's *Medical Jurisprudence* which stated that in order to convict the mother, or in this case Mrs Dennis, it was necessary to show that the child was willfully kept without food 'with the criminal intention of destroying it'. Mere neglect or imprudence would not make this a case of infanticide. The Coroner, Mr Carlyon left it to the jury to decide whether there had been sufficient evidence to justify them returning a verdict of murder or manslaughter against Dennis. The jury considered the matter, before returning a verdict that the child had died from the lack of improper care and insufficient food and from gross neglect. They added that in their opinion there was not sufficient evidence to warrant a verdict of murder or manslaughter. At the jury's request the woman Dennis was severely reprimanded by the Coroner and released. Once again the mother was thought culpable and not exempt from blame as Mr Carlyon added that 'with regard to the mother the jury thought she had been utterly wanting in that motherly affection for the child which she ought to have exhibited'. Hoping that was the end of the matter the two women left the Coroner's court.

But if Mary Dennis thought she had got away with it however she was wrong. The Truro Board of Guardians were so incensed at the decision that after the inquest they consulted with the police authorities. The outcome of the talks were that Mary Dennis was arrested the same night. She was brought before the Truro City Police Court on Saturday 17 November, charged with 'neglecting to provide food and care for an illegitimate male child which she had taken to nurse'. The story of the state of the child had been widespread in the town, and as a consequence the court room was crowded throughout the hearing. Mr R Marrack prosecuted Dennis on behalf of the Truro Board of Guardians. The first witness was Superintendent Angel who said that he had regularly passed the prisoner's house, and had seen notices in her window to the effect that she took in children to nurse. He described the inquest and how, following a reprimand, Todd and the mother had been set at liberty. The next to give evidence was the prisoner herself. Once again Dennis repeated the story that she had not sufficient money to provide better food for the child. Mr Richards corroborated the Superintendent's evidence and said that when he returned back to the workhouse, he gave the child to the porter, and immediately related the facts to the master of the workhouse. He told the court that he had a great deal of experience in such matters, but he had never seen anything so shocking before. Mr Sharp, the workhouse surgeon also described his visit, at the request of Superintendent Angel and Mr Richards, and he too spoke of his horror when he saw the child in such an emaciated state.

A lodger who lived at the house of Mary Dennis was a woman called Ann Lemon. She was the next to give her evidence, and she told the magistrates that she had lodged with the prisoner from 26 October to 9 November. She had gone to live with her as a result of her having an 'unsound leg' and expected Mary Dennis to nurse her. When she went to the house and realised there was also a baby on the premises, she told Dennis, that she could not possibly attend to both her and the child. Dennis promised to send the child away, but it remained. Mrs Lemon said that she was very disturbed by the child's cries, and that it always seemed hungry. To an almost silent court, the lodger then said that she only saw the prisoner feed it just once in 12 hours, and on one occasion just once in 24 hours. The food given to the child was bread and water and sometimes, but not very often, a little sugar was added to the mixture. When Mrs Lemon was reminded of the statement made by Dennis that the child had often refused food, she told the court that was not true. She added adamantly that she had never seen the child to be offered food and refused to take it, on the contrary, it was always anxious to have it. If she remonstrated with the prisoner for her callous attitude towards the child, the woman would swear at her and tell her to mind her own damn business. The witness claimed that she had once told Mrs Dennis 'the vengeance of the Almighty would rest upon her for her cruelty'.

Emily Bray then testified to being the mother of the child, and that she left him with the prisoner. She had paid Mary Dennis 3s 8d a week for its maintenance and sometimes she paid as much as 4s 6d. She had visited the child twice a week, and on the last occasion, a few days before it had died, she had complained that the child seemed thin. Mrs Dennis told her that she had called in a medical man who had given her some medicine, and she 'could do no more'. Countering the claim that she never paid Dennis enough money she told the magistrates that the woman had never complained to her that she did not pay her enough. Catherine Williams a nurse at the workhouse, stated that she had received the child in the evening of 7 November. The child was in a dirty and wretched condition and weighed only 5 lbs just before its death. She carefully bathed it before feeding him some sago, milk and sugar and the child managed to eat a little of it. The body was very blue, and stiff with cold and its skin was the colour of a plum. He had rallied a little bit, until early in the morning of 9 November when he died. When the prisoner was asked what she had to say in her defence, Dennis repeated her statement that the mother never gave her enough money for the child, and that as a consequence 'it must do without milk or sugar'. The chair to the magistrates, once again put the blame on the mother as he told the court:

'it was one of the worst cases that I have ever come across in the whole of my experience. The conduct of the mother as well as that of Dennis was unnatural, inhuman and utterly at variance with a mothers feelings or duty. She visited the house two or three time a week, saw what state the child was in, and yet never took any steps to improve its condition. I should have liked to have seen the mother standing at the side of the woman Dennis on a similar charge. I still hope that she might be punished in some way'.

He then ordered Dennis to take her trial at the next Quarter Sessions. Mary Dennis was brought before Sir Coleman Rashleigh and Mr A Coode at the Cornwall Epiphany Sessions on Tuesday 1 January 1878, where she was described as a housekeeper. The court heard the horrific details once again, before Dennis was sentenced to twelve months imprisonment with hard labour.

This case raises more questions than it answers. Why was there such a discrepancy in the amount of maintenance given to Dennis by the mother. It could be suggested that like many of the baby farmers in this book, that no services were offered for free. Perhaps the difference between 3s. 8d - 4s 6d stated by Bray and 1s 2d according to Dennis, was intended for the extra to pay for Emily Bray's upkeep at Dennis's house during her confinement. Like the chair to the magistrates, I cannot understand Bray's visiting the child after its birth, and saying nothing about its starving condition, which was obviously there for all to see. Also the statement of the lodger Mrs Lemon throws up more questions as to why, if she knew that the child was being starved had she said nothing to anyone. The most concerning part of the whole case was that if it wasn't for the neighbour's quarrel, this might be yet another uncounted death in the baby farming statistics.

Chapter Nine: John and Catherine Barnes

Most baby farmers preferred to work alone and in secret, but as we have already seen, when two people did work together, they tended to make a terrible duo. By now the numbers of baby farming cases that had been published in newspapers, encouraged this couple to develop to a fine art, elaborate lies to entrap women desperate to have their babies adopted. Learning from the reports, they also used a technique developed by many baby farmers to absolve themselves from blame. They too used the alibi that they had contracted out the babies for less money, disguising the true number of victims they had handled. All together it was thought that between 30 to 40 children had disappeared, after having being handed over to this particularly nasty couple. But the publicity given to baby farmers in the newspapers and the disgust that most people felt towards this evil trade, finally sounded the death knell to their career. It had been established as early as 1870 that a man and his wife, were engaged in this sordid trade around Liverpool and Birkenhead. Although several traps were set for them, each time the prisoners simply disappeared. They started again at a different addresses, operating under new names. Even though the police authorities knew that baby farming was being carried out under their noses, they were powerless to arrest them. In this manner they managed to evade the law for nine years, as they continued with their murderous activities.

By September 1879 the couple in question, John and Catherine Barnes, were at that time living on Church Road, Higher Tranmere, Birkenhead. As proof that the trade in which they engaged was lucrative, John Barnes appeared to live under a delusion of grandeur. To neighbour's and friends he gave off an air of gentility that belied his lowly position in society. He liked to present himself as a person of fashion and was known to visit acquaintances in a morning, not only dressed fashionably and smoking a good cigar, but usually the breast pocket of his suit was stuffed with banknotes. He had on several occasions borrowed money, which he usually paid back over a bottle of sparkling champagne. But his affluent lifestyle did not tie up with the squalor in which he, the children and his wife lived. After all the police authorities efforts to catch this couple, it was an unnamed gentleman from Sheffield, who finally brought them to heel. He had seen an advert in the local papers and had alerted the Liverpool police that there was a baby farm operating in Birkenhead. He had written to the couple in answer to an advert and it was agreed that they would meet at the Exchange Station in Liverpool, where the phantom baby would be exchanged. Mrs Barnes told the man from Sheffield that she would be dressed in black and her husband would wear a white hat with some black crepe around it in order that he would be able to identify them. After the meeting, the Sheffield man later identified the couple as Catherine and John Barnes. Now the police were confident that they had enough evidence to search the couples house but even in this they were frustrated.

When they approached a magistrate in the hope of getting a warrant from him, he refused. Even though the police now had evidence from witnesses who had heard the babies crying at the house, the magistrate refused to grant it on 'such flimsy evidence'. Inspector Clarke and several other officers were therefore forced to enter the house without a warrant on Wednesday 3 September 1879. They raided the house at 9 pm and demanded to see any children that might be there. Thankfully there was enough evidence in the many letters found at the house, to show the duplicity of the couple who sometimes called themselves Hall, Howell, Banks, Beard or Hamilton. One letter from John Barnes to a man in Hull stated that his wife 'was bent on having your boy' adding that 'I had a dream about him last night - a sweet dream'. Another claimed that Catherine and her husband 'moved through life in good society and had wealthy relatives', all of which was what parents wanted to hear for their child. In the kitchen they found three children, who they were told belonged to the couple, a girl aged 13 called Maria, and two other boys named John and Henry aged five and nine years. Mr Barnes said that they also had one child which they had only had for two months, and two others which had been with them for only one month. He claimed that he did not know where they came from and arrogantly added 'I will answer no other questions'. Catherine Barnes informed Inspector Clarke that there was another child upstairs, and he followed her up to the bedroom. There he found a girl in a dark and dirty room, where there was not a scrap of furniture. The child was naked apart from a rag wrapped around her middle and her body was covered in filth. The child did not cry as the woman and the officer approached, and Inspector Clarke formed the impression that she seemed to be not even strong enough to cry. He asked Mrs Barnes how long they had been baby farming, and she told him for nine years. Near the fireplace were some more rags on which he presumed the child had been lying. The woman told the police that child was called Florence and upon examination she proved to be the most emaciated of all of the children.

In the front room and lying upon a dirty mattress, were two other little children, although there were no blankets or sheets to cover them. Catherine told the Inspector that these two children were called Alice and Mabel, and the inspector noted that the mattress upon which they were lying was infested with fleas. All the children were badly neglected, wrapped in rags instead of clothing, and there was no food in the house apart from a loaf of bread. Despite John Barnes splendid clothes, the house itself was very poorly furnished and there were no bedclothes, even on the couple's own bed. A doctor was called, and he examined the smaller children, before having them sent straight to the Birkenhead workhouse. When the police searched the house, they found a total of 72 letters from desperate mothers, from such towns and cities as widespread as Manchester, Bristol and Rotherham. It was also established that the clothes which had been handed over with the children, were quickly pledged using various alias's at several of the local pawnshops. The following day, when the police went back to the house they took the three older children, Maria, John and Henry also into the workhouse.

On Thursday 4 September 1879 John aged 41 and Catherine Barnes aged 28 were brought into the Police Court at the Birkenhead Town Hall. They were charged with neglecting to provide sufficient nourishment to three of the children in their care. The names of the children was given as Alice Mabel Emily Hamilton aged 5 months. The child known only as Mabel aged 7 months and Florence aged 23 months. The magistrate Mr Preston, had been informed only that morning, that Mabel, had died in the workhouse and told the couple they were now facing charges of wilful murder. The other two children were still reported to be in a very dangerous condition, and it was uncertain whether they would survive. He emphasized the seriousness of the case, when he told the other magistrates that 'as many as ten children had been placed in their care since January, and only three could be accounted for'. The prisoners stated that even they could not account for the missing children, due to the fact that they had been farmed out to other persons for a lesser fee. Inspector Clarke asked for a remand for a week. He explained that several letters which had been found at the house, needed to be followed up in order to try to establish exactly how many children the couple had 'adopted' by this method. He also told the court that in order to gain as much evidence as possible, they were in communication with ten or twelve different police authorities, all of which took time. The magistrate agreed, stating that he doubted these would be the last cases of baby farming that he would hear from that area, as the Infant Life Protection Act of 1872 was not in force in Birkenhead. This Act made the registration with the local authority compulsory, for persons taking in and charging for two or more children for a period of more than 24 hours. It was also compulsory that the name of any child that died, had to be given to the Coroner within 24 hours of the death. However because the Birkenhead Local Authority did not recognise the Act, it rendered the requirements useless.

The two prisoners were remanded until Wednesday 17 September, but the next court appearance was also very brief, as the police authorities were still pursuing their enquiries. The publication of the stories of the callousness of the couple towards the children in their care had angered local people. They were hissed at and booed on their way to and from the courthouse. The two prisoners complained to the magistrate that they were also being insulted inside prison, and were not allowed pen and ink to write to friends. Inspector Clarke assured the court that they had been given every opportunity to write any letters that they wished. Feelings were still very high as the prisoners were being brought into court, and such was the hatred towards them, that the couple must have feared for their lives. However once safely established in the courtroom they appeared arrogant and superior. The prosecution Mr Moore explained the delay when he warned the court that the police have been dealing with such a large number of missing children 'that when the whole case was complete, such a history of crime would be brought to light that was almost unprecedented'. The couple were again remanded until Saturday 20 September.

When they again arrived at the court that day, they were told by the prosecution Mr Moore that the baby called Alice had died. He said that she had been handed over to the female prisoner on 18 July. Mr Moore told the court that police officers had been looking at the local cemeteries and that several deaths of children who had lived previously with the prisoners, were said to be buried at the Birkenhead and Bebington graveyards. According to their records there was a seven month old child called Ellen Bradbury, who had been buried on 5 September 1878 when the couple lived at Helmington Road. It had been at that address that another child, a boy registered as William Barnes aged 21 months had died and been buried by them on the 18 September 1878. A third child, Ethel Russell aged four years, was also buried on 21 January of the present year, when they were living at Walker Street, Tranmere. Mr Moore added that the registers of all three deaths had been signed by Mrs Catherine Barnes. He stated that because of the numbers of children involved, the enquiry had taken on such major implications that the Treasury had decided to take over the case. Because of that Mr Moore said that he intended to call only sufficient witnesses to justify a further remand. Mr Williams, the master of the Birkenhead workhouse, testified to the death of the two children Mabel and Alice. Dr Laidlaw, the medical officer for the workhouse, testified that the cause of death in both cases was long and sustained malnutrition. He told the court that the third child called Florence was still in a very poorly state, and she was not expected to live for much longer. Dr Laidlaw said that two children that had been removed from the house were, at present alive and well, and that great efforts were being made by the police to trace their parents. The problems they had experienced in tracing the children 'adopted' by the couple, had been made more difficult by the fact that the two prisoners had used many alias's in their dealings. They had used the name of Howell, Hall, Banks, Beard and Hamilton. Nevertheless it had been established that Barnes was their real name. Then the couple were once more remanded.

An inquest on the two children known only as Alice and Mabel was opened on Friday 19 September, in front of the Coroner, Mr Henry Churton. The Coroner told the jury that there were still many concerns about the other children that had been taken to the workhouse. Because of that he was intending to adjourn the inquest until after a post mortem could be held, which might elicit more information. He warned the jury that they may very well soon be investigating a third death, as the child Florence was still very ill. He mentioned the fourteen year old girl Maria, who had been adopted by the couple was still in the workhouse and several of the jurymen expressed a wish to talk to the girl. However the Coroner thought that she 'was a poor weak, ignorant girl whose evidence would not materially affect the case' before adjourning the inquest. On Wednesday 25 September 1879 the inquest was resumed and the first witness was Alice Maria Rodenhurst who lived in Hereford. She said she was the mother of the child Alice who had been born on 15 April, and handed over to the female prisoner at Hereford Station on May 17. Miss Rodenhurst admitted having advertised in a Liverpool newspaper for someone to adopt the child. The witness told the police that a bundle of clothes had been handed over at the same time, which she had identified from clothing found at the house after the prisoners had been taken into custody. The arrangement she had made with the woman, was that she would give her £30 to bring up the child as her own, and the money was handed over. When she was contacted by the police she had identified the child at the workhouse, and like other mothers before her could hardly recognized her child, which had been healthy and strong when she was handed it to the female prisoner.

A woman called Ellen Long then gave evidence that she had been at a confinement house where unmarried mothers gave birth in Leeds. On 20 April a single woman called Emma Green had given birth to the child called Mabel, before having her adopted in order to go to Manchester, where she had found a position in service. The witness told the court that she had kept the child with her until 19 July, as the father was paying 7s a week for its keep. But she agreed with the father that it would be better if the child be handed over for adoption. Ellen Long stated that she had advertised the child for adoption, and had received a reply from Mr and Mrs Barnes, using the name Hall. A meeting was arranged and the child had been handed over. Long told the Coroner that the child was well dressed when she gave it to Catherine Barnes, and that two or three changes of clothes had also been given to the prisoner. She too identified some of the clothing which had been recovered from one of the many pawn shops, where they had been deposited by the prisoners. Ellen Long had been told that 'Mrs Hall' and her husband already had a son, but that they now wanted to adopt a little girl. Samuel Blythe of Wigan said he knew the mother of Mabel, and when he saw an advert from a couple calling themselves Hall, he was invited to the house to meet them. When he arrived at the house, the woman was on her own and she told him that she had a son aged seven who was at school. Blythe told the Coroner that more letters passed between them and that the prisoner had originally asked for £30 for the adoption, but they finally agreed on £10. The child was handed over and he was assured that she would be loved and brought up in a religious manner. The Coroner commented that it seemed very strange that a child should be handed over for a sum as small as ten pounds, but the witness told him that 'Mrs Hall' gave the impression that she was taking the child out of affection, rather than for the money.

The Coroner summed up for the jury stating that the evidence proved that the two prisoners were solely in charge of the children, and they were responsible for what happened to them. Given the poorly state of the children when they had been found, they could not have disguised from themselves the fact that the children were ill. He pointed out bluntly to the jury that the couple had taken the children under false representation, and they had allowed those children to suffer to the point of death. The jury took just half an hour to find them both guilty of wilful murder. The Coroner ordered that they were to be sent to take their trial at the assizes, and told them that it was one of the worst cases he had to deal with. Before they could appear at the assizes however, on Thursday 25 September, the prisoners were once again brought back before the magistrate charged with the murder of the third child known as Florence, who had since died at the workhouse. Mr Moore was once again prosecuting on the behalf of the Treasury, and he said that there were now sixteen or seventeen charges against the prisoners. In reply to letters answering the adverts, they wrote such letters, which contained nothing but lies. He brought one of the letters to the court and read it out for the jury. It said:

'We are in receipt of your letter in answer to our advertisement. I beg to state we will be happy to treat with you for the little orphan and can only say the little one will have a good home, under the kind treatment of Christian people, and will never know or learn anything by us but love and affection. Our earnest prayers will be that the little one should grow to be a blessing to us in life and always brighten our fireside. As regards the premium, shall we say forty pounds to take the little one over as our own begotten child for its natural life? We have had other applications and should be glad to hear from you as soon as possible, stating when the little one could be had. Of course the little one being left motherless, we have given it our first consideration, it being one of Christ's little ones.'

Mr Moore said that was just one of countless letters that had been found at the house and several others had been found on the person of the girl Maria when she was taken to the workhouse. The evidence of the next door neighbour's and his wife was given. Andrew Morton stated that he and his wife were kept awake during the night, by constant crying of a child in the back room of the house. The sound that the child made, gave the impression that it was in great pain. Mrs Morton told the court that when she had asked the female prisoner about the child crying, she said merely said that 'it was ill and was being treated by Doctor Jones of Birkenhead'. Her husband said the crying was often as much as two or three times in an hour, and that he had witnessed both prisoners going in and out of the house next door. He thought that the male prisoner had no employment, but despite that he always dressed as a dandy. Neither of the prisoners made any remarks on the new charge, but it was commented that the female prisoner at times seemed to enjoy the proceedings, as she smiled to herself as the evidence was being heard. Nevertheless flashes of anger also erupted and it was noted that she had to be restrained by her husband and her solicitor, as she challenged the witnesses giving their evidence. It was at this point that the case was adjourned to the following day.

When the magistrates court reconvened the bench was treated to yet another catalogue of horrific stories about the mothers and children involved in this case. The first witness was a young woman who introduced herself as Elizabeth Ann Thompson of Heckmondwike, near Halifax and she told the court she was a domestic servant. She had been confined of a female child at the Wakefield workhouse on 14 October of the previous year. Having finally gained a position, Miss Thompson had put the baby out to nurse six months after its birth. Subsequently she saw an advert in the Bradford newspapers and wrote to the given address. In reply she received a letter from a person giving the name of Hampson and went to meet both the prisoners at Wakefield station. Thompson said that she had signed a form to say that she would give them her baby and 'she should not annoy them afterwards about it'. She paid them £9 and handed over the baby which, at the time, the baby was well dressed and well cared for. She had later sent a hamper of clothes for the child, which she had been instructed to send to the station, writing on the hamper that it was 'to be called for'. The witness told the court that she had recently seen the same baby in the possession of a woman called Mrs Devine, and had barely recognised it as her own. Mrs Devine appeared in court and told them that she had been handed the baby from the prisoners. They had paid her £1 deposit and they promised to pay her 5s a week, but they had only paid her 8s in total before the money stopped altogether. When Mrs Devine remonstrated with the female prisoner she came and took the baby away, but on the 7 July she brought it back in such an emaciated state, that even Mrs Devine herself was shocked. She told the court that since that time she had not received any money from the prisoners, and had to give up her position to look after the child herself. As a consequence she had been forced to pawn her own clothes to keep the baby in food and pay the rent.

Inspector Clarke said that they had found a number of letters at the house which had been sent by mothers enquiring about their children. One letter had been found that had been written by Catherine Barnes in reply to an enquiry about a child that had been adopted by them. She wrote that at that time the child had been ill and 'they were not taking the little one out, as they were trying to keeping it warm'. Inspector Clarke revealed the couple's duplicity, when he told the court that at the time this letter had been sent to the anxious mother, the baby's clothes were already in the pawn shop. Another letter which had been sent to the prisoners from a mother wanting to see her child, had forced them to retrieve it from its new foster mother, in order to be able to show it to the actual mother. The next witness was a domestic servant called Emma Bates from Bath. She told the court that on

13 May she had been delivered of a male child, and about three weeks later she saw an advertisement in a Bristol paper. She had met the female prisoner at Lime Street Station, and she had tea with her and her husband. Barnes told her that he would look after the baby and bring it up so well that one day it would be famous, telling her that 'one day she will see its name in the newspapers' which produced some rare laughter in the court room. Miss Bates had paid £10 to the Barnes to have her baby adopted, and thankfully it had been discovered still alive. She told the court how she had gone to Birkenhead the previous week, and was notified by the police that they had found her baby at Manchester. She was shown and identified some of the clothing which she had given to the couple, which had been pawned. Another woman called Lucy Jones next gave evidence that she had adopted the same baby for £5 from Catherine Barnes, and that she had become very attached to the child. The magistrates at this point adjourned the case for a further period. It was reported that throughout the trial the male prisoner maintained his haughty demeanor, whilst the woman remained 'sly and stubborn' throughout.

On the same day that the prisoners were brought before the police court once again on Wednesday 31 September 1879, it was announced that because of the disgust around this case, the Birkenhead Town Council had now agreed to adopt the Infant Life Protection Act for the Borough. The girl who was thought to be the couple daughter than gave her evidence. She said her name was Maria Louisa Walker and her parents lived at Leeds and she knew that she had been adopted by Mr and Mrs Barnes. The girl claimed that she had been with them since 1873, and had been adopted when it was established that she would inherit £1,200 when she reached the age of 21 years. The girl testified that under her adopted mothers instructions, she had regularly taken the children clothes to the pawn shop. She also admitted that when she had been taken to the workhouse, she was found to have several other letters addressed to other people, concealed in her frock. She appeared dressed in workhouse garb and she described how she had nursed the babies. The girl claimed that in her care the children she helped to look after, were all well fed and had plenty to eat. Mr Moore told the court that enquiries were still being made into the other two boys, who also claimed to be the offspring of the prisoners, and were still being cared for at the workhouse. He told the court that the police were also making many enquiries into the discovery of the numbers of dead children, that had been found in the vicinity of the different houses where the couple had lived. Mr Moore stated that the body of a young male child had been found on the doorstep of a house on Bridge Street, Birkenhead near to where the couple had rented a property. At the inquest on the little body a verdict had been returned that the unnamed child had simply been 'found dead'. A similar discovery of a little boy was made on 1 January 1879 in Birkenhead Park by one of the gardeners, and at that inquest the jury recorded an open verdict. The prosecution stated that they now believed that both those deaths were attributable to the prisoners. In 1877 they gave away a baby for adoption to a couple in Tattenhall, a village near Chester, but the baby was in such a weak condition that it soon died. A letter had since been sent to the police station claiming that the baby had died of starvation.

Mr Moore gave evidence about the child Florence, and then the magistrate stated that he would remand the prisoners to the next day, when they would be committed to the assizes. He explained that the biggest difficulties experienced in this particular case, as well as in many other cases of the same type, was because most if not all of the babies, had been born illegitimately. Because of the secrecy around the birth the parents were reluctant to come forward, so it was impossible to identify all the children. On Wednesday 1 October 1879 the prisoners were back in court. It was noted that as the couple came into the courtroom, there was an audible hissing and booing as they took their place in the dock. The defence tried to provide witnesses to show that the children had been properly cared for. Sarah Minx, the wife of a milk dealer, stated that milk was had been regularly supplied to the house, and sometimes they had bread and other food delivered. A lodger, a woman called Ann Gibbons stated that she had lodging in a room at the prisoners house from September 1878 to May 1879 and remembered the child Florence coming to them. She told the magistrate that she was a fine healthy child, but had soon fallen ill with measles, and she declined in health after that. The magistrate heard all the evidence, before stating that he was now going to commit the prisoners for trial at the assizes on the charge of wilfully murdering two of the children called Mabel and Alice. In the case of the child called Florence the prisoner would merely be charged with a misdemeanor. When they were asked if they had anything to say, Catherine Barnes denied the charges, and replied that she had 'always made myself a perfect slave for the children'.

On Tuesday October 28 1879 the two prisoners were tried before Lord Justice Brett at the Chester Assizes. Defence witness, Maria Louisa Walker again stated that the babies were fed milk and bread twice a day and sometimes more, and they were always covered up when they were asleep. She did however admit that the child Florence was sometimes put into the back room and left to cry. The female prisoner swooned whilst Mr McIntyre addressed the jury for the prosecution, but after being given some water she seemed to recover a little. After hearing from witnesses throughout a very long day, the case was adjourned until the following morning. The next day there was once again so many witnesses that the trial didn't end until 8 pm. After listening to all the witnesses the judge then gave his conclusions. He said that although the police had found two children on the only bed in house, the inference was that all three were usually laid, nearly naked on bundles of foul straw. He said the fact that 'such young children were left to fester in such an abomination could hardly to be described. The children had all died of starvation and the want of attention'. Justice Brett warned the jury not to let their feelings carry them beyond what the law would justify, when they made their verdict. The prisoners could not be found guilty of wilful murder unless it was shown that they intended to cause death, but a verdict of 'want of reasonable care' would be the same as manslaughter. The jury found both prisoners guilty of manslaughter and the judge told them that they had 'for years and years carried on the vilest trade that human malignity could have invented'.

Mr Justice Brett, like many judges before him of the period, then place some of the blame on the parents themselves. He spoke at some length upon the foolishness and wickedness of 'those people who placed children with such as the prisoners' which was a reflection on the feelings of the society at the time. The judge warned John and Catherine Barnes that 'they had been within a hairs breadth of murder' before he sentenced them both to penal servitude for life. On 5 November it was announced that a letter had been received from Catherine Barnes at Birkenhead demanding to see her own children before she was to be removed from Chester Gaol. In the letter she stated that 'it is perhaps through loving them more than God, that has brought her to the condition in which she was now placed'. The letter continued:

'The cruel enemies of my husband and myself have done all they could against them, but they cannot deprive them of the Kingdom of Heaven. I took charge of eight children altogether, but some of them were returned and two are now in good homes. I will not live a week if I do not see the children before I go'.

It is not recorded whether she was granted permission to see her children, but it seems that throughout the trial this couple lived in a fantasy world of their own making. Despite the squalour of their surroundings they treated other people, including the legal authorities, as lesser mortals and refused to accept their guilt. In condemning John and Catherine Barnes Justice Brett blamed the parents whose children had died, but research indicates that many of these mothers of illegitimate children, really wanted to believed the lies that the baby farmers told them. They desperately wanted to believe that their children would be adopted by a respectable and loving couple. Combine that with a plausible pair of loathsome fraudsters who told them what they wanted to hear, these desperate women were far from 'foolish and wicked', as they handed over their children.

Chapter Ten: Annie Tooke

It was not just lonely, friendless working girls that had illegitimate children in Victorian society. Although it was less common, sometimes it was a middle class woman, who with the support of her family gave birth. Such a woman was Mary Hoskins of Camborne, Cornwall. Along with her brother and sister they contrived to keep the birth of the baby away from their aged parents. It was only when the child was found horribly mutilated, did the truth become known. The mother in this case was forced to break the truth to her parents, that not only had she given birth to an illegitimate son, but she had been arrested for the murder of the child.

Mary Hoskins was a single woman aged 25 years who lived with her parents, who were both in their early sixties. Her father was very respectable and had belonged to the Hayle family, who was well known in the area of Camborne. He was a mining engineer and he worked with mining machines in Italy for many years, until he had a seizure and became ill. Once his health became delicate, his daughter accompanied him on his travels. She had been brought up by her parents to be a respectable young woman, who was described as being 'a ladylike and a gentle mannered girl of good appearance'. Nevertheless in 1879 she found herself to be pregnant by a man called Reginald who was an accountant. Without the knowledge of her parents, she arranged to go away to have the baby. In order for it not to be known in Camborne, she had taken lodgings at a little village about two miles from Exeter called Ide, in May 1878. She was accompanied by a man she called Mr Hooper, who she said was her brother. The couple took furnished rooms with a Mr Johnson, to whom she told her name was Hede and that she was married, although her husband was at present out of England. The rooms were paid for by Mr Hooper, who told Mr Johnson that he would visit his sister once a month, but in actual fact it was nearer to ten weeks before he returned.

Naturally in a little village there was much talk about the strange woman who appeared to be pregnant, and was surmised that she was probably not married and had given a false name. However Mrs Hede was so refined and gentle that neighbour's grew to like her and suspicion of her was lulled. She was also an able seamstress and when her brother finally came to visit her, he brought materials for her to sew. It was also noted by neighbour's that Mrs Hede also received plenty of mail, and every week she picked up a large package from the Post Office. The post mistress noted that she would write many letters after this package had been delivered. The Vicar of Ide found her to be a very religious young woman, who regularly attended church, and he invited her to become a member of a bible class. Neighbour's also noted that as the date of the birth drew near, she had plenty of clothes for the child, which again had been brought by the brother. It was noted that the baby clothes were not new, although they were of very good quality. Mrs Hede hired a medical man, Dr Webb of Exeter about the end of July or the beginning of August. She was also attended by a professional nurse called Mary Jane Downe. The child was born at some time in October and was said to be 'a full grown healthy little boy' although it was stated that he had some form of deformity on his 'member'.

The child was registered on 7 November and given the name, Reginald Hede. After his birth, Mrs Hede intimated to her landlord Mr Johnson that she would soon be leaving Ide, although she promised to return for a visit. Her brother came on the Saturday 9 November, accompanied by a married sister called Mrs Elizabeth Tonkin. All three slept at Mr Johnson's that night in order to make an early start in the Sunday morning, when they left for Exeter. The brother, Mr Hooper had been making enquiries into a suitable nurse in whose care to leave the baby, and he was given the name of Annie Tooke, who nursed children. On the morning they left Ide Hooper took a cab to the station, whilst Mrs Tonkin accompanied her sister to the house of Mrs Tooke, where they left the child before returning back to Camborne. Back at her parents house the story that had been given out was that Mary Hoskins had been staying with relatives, and the plan worked so well that even her own parents were not aware that their daughter had given birth. A few months later however their carefully constructed plan was about to be blown apart.

The following year on the 17 May 1879 the mutilated remains of a child was found in a parcel, recovered from a mill pond by a man employed at a nearby flour mill on Bonhay Road, Exeter. To his horror, as he unwrapped the bundle he saw that he had found the trunk of a small child whose limbs had been cut off and the head decapitated. A photograph had been taken of the face of the child and had been shown around by police officers to those women of Ide that looked after children. Annie Tooke admitted that it looked very much like a child that she had nursed, which had been taken away on 12 May. A Coroner's inquest was held on 21 May and Annie Tooke was called to give evidence. She told the Coroner that the child had been entrusted to her care by a woman calling herself Mrs Hede on 10 November 1878. She was asked how long she had the child in her care and she said until the 12 May 1879 when 'someone came and took the baby away'. She said that she had agreed to be paid 5s a week and had been given £12 in advance, and the child's mother had promised to send more clothes for the baby. She had also given her a paper with permission to get the child vaccinated. When Tooke was questioned about the woman who had taken the child away, she described her as having a veil over her face, although she claimed that she would be able to identify her again. Tooke stated that the woman had just turned up one day, and asked if she still had the child. Tooke said that she had, and that's when the woman informed her that she had come to take it away. Tooke asked where the mother was and she said that she was in town buying some clothes for the child. The child was then removed and she had heard no more of it since.

The police surgeon, Mr Charles Edward Bell gave evidence that he had conducted a post mortem on the remains. He told the stunned court that the child had been killed by a blow to the back of the head, and then its throat had been cut, allowing it to bleed to death. The mark on its head which was about the size of a shilling, looked almost like a hammer blow. When he completed the post mortem he found that the child had been fed within an hour or a half hour before its death. The Chief Constable of Plymouth, Captain Bent gave evidence that the child had not been vaccinated, and he made enquiries in the city of Exeter and various parts of North Devon. The jury offered a verdict of wilful death against 'a person or persons unknown'. Village gossip of the remains of the child soon reached the ears of Mr Scanes, a butcher who had lived next door to Mr Johnson. He was familiar with the child, as he had lived next door to it for four or five weeks after it had been born and was aware that the boy had a deformity on his private parts. He questioned the cabman who had driven Mrs Hede and her brother and sister away from Ide. The cabman told him that when he picked up his passengers, he had been instructed to go to the home of Mrs Tooke, who at that time occupied three attic rooms on Bartholomew Street, Ide. Mr Scanes told Dr Webb about deformation on the child's member and they both agreed that the child which had been mutilated was that of Reginald Hede. He told the doctor that he needed to speak to Mrs Tooke who was staying at the Volunteer Inn, and he accompanied the doctor there. They found Mrs Tooke, who was aged about forty and who had several other children that she was also looking after, with her. She repeated the story that she had looked after little Reginald Hede, but that a stranger had come and taken the child away. They questioned her about the boy and asked her whether it had some deformity or not, which she totally denied.

Mr Scanes then went to the police and told them his story and his suspicions around the Mrs Tooke and the woman known as Mrs Hede. It had been noted that the woman known as Mrs Hede had sent some letters which she addressed to her brother, Mr Hooper 'care of Mr Tonkin, chemist of Camborne'. Captain Bent therefore lost no time in sending one of his men, Inspector Short to Camborne in Cornwall. There Inspector Short and Sergeant Beare of the Camborne police quickly found that the woman known as Mrs Hede was in fact a young unmarried woman called Mary Hoskins. She was arrested on a charge of murder and removed by a cab to Exeter. On Saturday 7 June 1879 the case of Mary Hoskins was heard at the Exeter Guildhall by six magistrates. She was charged with being an accessory before the fact in the murder of her infant son, Reginald Hede between 12 and 17 May. Now that her shameful secret had been revealed, the court was jam packed as Mary Hoskins took her place. It was reported that she wore a light coloured jacket over a black silk dress, and on her head she sported a black hat with a feather and a heavy veil covering her face. Hoskins remained standing whilst the Chief Constable was making his statement, and she was leaning upon the rail of the dock for support, while at the same time attempting to screen herself as much as possible. Annie Tooke told the court that from November to her arrest, Mary Hoskins had not attempted to visit her child, nor seemed to show any interest in it. She described how a woman had arrived to pick up the child about 3.30 pm on 12 May. The woman had asked her if she was nursing a child and Tooke admitted that she was. When the magistrate asked that Mary Hoskins be remanded to the next week, in the prisoner's naivety she asked him 'couldn't it be finished now'. The magistrate told her 'that was not how the legal system worked' and she was removed.

Police enquiries however uncovered a different story. After further remands of the prisoner the case was finally resumed on Friday 13 June, when both Annie Tooke and Mary Hoskins were both stood in the dock with a female warder in between them. The prosecution was opened by Mr Walter Friend who placed the whole of the blame on the baby farmer for the murder of the child. He stated that Tooke had taken charge of the child in November for which she was paid £12 in advance. He told the court that once the money ran out, Tooke applied for some more and when she found that the mother had no interest in the child, she decided to do away with it. She had written a letter to her sister in Plymouth complaining about the 'poor, miserable child' and the amount of food it consumed. Mr Friend stated that when the police searched Tooke's rooms, they found an old tin box with several dents in it. He alleged that was where the baby farmer had cut up the child's body on the box. Blood stained flannel and clothing were also found at her house, as well as a razor and a chopper. As the prosecution continued to outlined the case, Hoskins sobbed and appeared to be in great distress, as she heard the gruesome details of what had happened to her son. At this point her solicitor Mr Henry Rogers asked that his client, who was obviously innocent of the charge of murder, should be dismissed. It would seem that both the magistrate and the prosecution Mr Friend agreed, and as she left the court in almost a semi conscious state, she was cheered. Annie Tooke was remanded.

On Wednesday June 18 the Exeter Guildhall was reported to be crammed in every part to see the woman who had killed a child in such a brutal fashion. The prosecution, Mr Friend pointed out that when the child's mother had showed no interest in the child, he claimed that was when Tooke had made up her mind to dispose of it. He informed the magistrates that to hide her tracks, the prisoner had changed her accommodation on three different occasions. He pointed out that the last known address had been on South Street, Ide which was only a short distance to the mill pond where the child's body had been found. When other lodgers missed the child, she told them that she had placed it with another nurse for 4s a week. Mary Hoskin's sister, Mrs Tonkin appeared, and spoke about how she had handed over the money to Tooke. She also requested that she did not try to get in touch with her sister in the future. When cross examined on this point, she stated that she did not want anyone in Camborne to know that her sister had an illegitimate child. She also said that on many occasions her sister had wanted to visit the child, but she had persuaded her to leave it until his first birthday. Tooke was found guilty and sent to take her trial for the murder of Reginald Hede. The next day she sent for the Chief Constable and she told him that she wanted to make a confession. He advised her to take legal advice before she did, but Tooke told him that 'she supposed someone would be hung for the murder'. She told him that she had smothered the child with a pillow, before dismembering it to avoid recognition. Tooke added that she had murdered the child and that no one else had anything to do with it, and then signed the confession. However she had changed her mind the next day, and wrote a letter to the police authorities stating that the confession she had made was false. She now claimed that she had in fact given the child to a woman she met in the street, and asked her to take it to the workhouse.

The trial started on Monday 21 July 1879 at the Exeter Guildhall for the murder of Reginald Hede aged 6 months in front of Mr Justice Lopes. When Tooke was asked how she pleaded she replied that she was not guilty. She was assisted in a half fainting condition into the court by a warder and the prison school mistress. Throughout the hearing 'the proceedings were interrupted by her hysterical attacks of crying, which, although not of a long duration, were violent and painful to witness'. Mrs Tonkin gave evidence that she had visited her sister whilst she was at Ide with her brother, and she had seen that she was very fond of the baby. She told the court that it was only with great difficulty that she was induced to part with the little boy, and hand him over to Mrs Tooke. Mrs Tonkin had also noted the malformation of the little boy's private parts, and had mentioned it to the doctor. She also stated that from the time that the baby had been handed over, her sister had not left Camborne and the home of her parents. The next witness was a man called Henry Satchell who was a pawnbroker. He stated that on 24 June the daughter of the prisoner had come to his shop to pawn a baby's shawl. On 31 January the same girl had pawned a child's white robe. It was noted that when Tooke had been arrested, that she had many pawn tickets for children clothing on her person. Two witnesses gave evidence that she had left the lodgings at 61 South Street between 8 pm and 9 pm on the night before the baby's body was found in the mill pool. Inspector Short spoke about the search he had made on her rooms, and he described finding the box. At this point the case was adjourned until the following day, as it had already lasted seven hours.

On Tuesday 22 July 1879 Tooke was again brought into the court and she appeared to be much more composed than she had the previous day. Captain Bent spoke about the remains of the baby being found, and how it had been brought in to the police station on 18 May. He described photographing the child's face and Tooke admitting that it was the child she had cared for. The judge gave a summary of the evidence for the jury, who retired at 6.05 pm and returned an hour later to find Annie Tooke guilty of murder. The judge in passing sentence told her that 'I would have been astonished had the jury arrived at any different conclusion'. He then assumed the black cap, as he passed the sentence of death. On Monday August 11 Annie Tooke was hanged at Exeter gaol. It was said that her four children visited her on the Saturday, and she was hanged by Marwood the executioner. It was a private execution held in the prison hospital, but members of the press were admitted to the inquest afterwards. At the inquest which was held at noon, the governor of the prison Major Kirkpatrick read out her confession which stated:

'I hereby acknowledge that the confession I made to Captain Bent is true in the main particulars; that I am justly to suffer for my dreadful crime for which, as for all my many sins, I do most truly repent and heartily pray God's mercy, for the sake of his dear Son, my only Lord and Saviour, Jesus Christ. Signed by me. ANNIE TOOKE'

The confession which had been written on the morning of August 9 was witnessed by the matron of Exeter Gaol, Mrs S A Hughes and the governor Mr Sutton Kilpatrick.

Chapter Eleven: Alice Reeves

As the numbers of baby farmers increased, the authorities recognised that the Infant Life Protection Act of 1872 had done nothing to stop this vile trade. Bodies of children continued to be found on the streets of the cities and towns of Britain. Thankfully a society had been formed in 1884 which would shine a light on the activities of these baby farmers. They appointed inspectors whose specific brief was to look into the cases of the neglect of children. This was the Society for the Prevention of Cruelty to Children which had been formed in London, and was renamed a National Society in 1889 when branches were opened up in most towns and cities. Now this Society, not only had the authority to check out cases of abuse (involving parents as well as baby farmers) but they also had the power to prosecute them. Finally people were beginning to see the death knell to this despicable business. This case also illustrates how baby farmers, were not just content to take the few shillings to care for a child, but they would also try to extort money out of them for doctors fees.

Alice Reeves was 40 years old in December 1890 and like most baby farmers she was a heartless killer, who callously watched babies die in front of her eyes. For many years the police had been on her trail, but like others before her, she changed her name and address with such frequency they were unable to catch her. Her pattern of behaviour was such that her tenancy in the different houses never lasted longer than three months, before she left the premises often owing rent. However, unlike Reeves, her neighbour's could not shut their eyes and ears to the cries of hungry children, and it was for this reason alone that she was finally caught. When Reeves opened the door of her latest rented house at Eastlake Road, Camberwell, South London in the afternoon of 30 December 1890, she found three men on her doorstep. They were Police Sergeant Cockerell and Dr Frank Reid and Inspector David Patton of the NSPCC, who were visiting the house following a complaint made by a neighbour. The men rang the bell several times, but there was no answer. Sergeant Cockerell went to a downstairs door and knocked, and it was finally answered by a girl. He asked if Reeves was in and the girl replied in the affirmative and invited him into the house. They walked along a passage, past the front parlour and into a small kitchen at the back of the house. Inside Reeves was sitting with two other women trying to pacify a small child, whilst four other children were sitting or lying around on chairs. The house was a small terraced house with little furniture particularly in the ground floor, back kitchen where the children were kept. To his horror Dr Frank Reid found all five of the children were groaning and in obvious distress. Also at the house was a man called Charles Stanley May, a solicitor who had been living with Reeves. PC Cockerell asked Reeves if she was a baby farmer and she hotly denied it, stating indignantly that she was a nurse. He asked Reeves how many children she had in the house and she told him 'I have these children you see here, and another two in the other room'. She claimed they were all the illegitimate children of her daughters, Frances and Eleanor who, until a day or so before, had lived with her.

She told Sergeant Cockerell that the child Nelly belonged to her daughter Eleanor and she was subject to fits. She claimed that Albert Reeves was Frances's child, but she declined to tell him how long she had taken care of any of the children. Another boy was called

Stephen Simmons aged 6 months and Reeves admitted that he was the child she was caring for, as his mother was traveling with a lady in Switzerland. At first she claimed that all the other children belonging to her. There was a boy called Lewis, aged 1 year and 8 months, and a girl, Louise May Reeves was aged 13 months. As Reeves was identifying the children in the room, two more children came in, who she reluctantly told Inspector Patton were Florence and Agnes Fletcher. After some more badgering from the inspector, she claimed their father was a traveller of some kind, but she had no idea of his whereabouts. Sergeant Cockerell asked her if there were any more children in the house, and she told him that there was another child upstairs, but that it had 'nothing to do with her'. She was accompanied upstairs by the police sergeant who found the bedroom contained four cribs and a cradle, all holding filthy mattresses. In the room was a boy aged about fourteen, who she said was her own child and he was holding a smaller child. The boy's name was Ernest Reeves and the child was Adrian Brown who was about two months old. Dr Reid examined all the children and found them to be very emaciated, and he ordered some milk to be brought to the house. Once the milk had been delivered and was being fed to the children, they drank it ravenously. Meanwhile Inspector Patton searched the house and found many children's garments. He later reported that some of them looked to be expensively made.

Three days later on 2 January 1891, Reeves opened her door to Inspector Daniel Sullivan of P division, who carried with him a warrant. When he showed her the warrant for her arrest on the charge of child neglect, she typically tried to blame everyone except herself. Reeves told him

'I have not willfully neglected the kids. it is a shame, there is a conspiracy against me. It is that Dr Simpson because I have not paid him. I have done my best for the children, I have not slept for three nights whilst I have been attending them. I took one to the hospital three weeks ago but they would not take it in'.

When arrested she told him 'I have said too much, I shall not say any more. You will have to find out'. Inspector Sullivan searched the house and eight of the children; Nelly, Albert, Lewis, Louise, Stephen, Adrian, Florence and Agnes were removed to a shelter of the NSPCC at Harper Street, Holborn. Six of the eight children were found to be in such an emaciated condition that, it was felt by Dr Reid that they could not have survived in the house for much longer. On Friday 9 January 1891 Alice Reeves was brought before the Lambeth Magistrates Court before Mr Biron QC, where she was charged with having so grossly neglected six of the children in her care 'as to cause them unnecessary suffering and injury'. Inspector Patton prosecuted the case on behalf of the NSPCC and he told the court how, following the unnamed neighbours complaint, they had gone to the house and found the children.

Police enquiries into the case had established that the prisoner regularly advertised for children to take charge of, or adopt. Neighbours stated that several ladies had been seen to go to the house, carrying infants and exiting without them. The police were at that time trying to locate all the parents of the children in the house. Dr Reid gave evidence that he had visited four of the children, now in the shelter, and found them much improved. He stated that when the children were removed they were all found to be seriously underweight, and one of them Stephen Simmons was in a very serious condition indeed. The magistrates had no option, but to remand the prisoner. Sadly, later that day it was announced that Stephen had died. On Tuesday 13 January 1891 the inquest was held on the body of Stephen Simmons was heard in front of Coroner Dr G Danford Thomas at Holborn Town Hall. The legal authorities, used to dealing with baby farmers, were becoming more understanding about not revealing the names of the mothers of the illegitimate children. Because of this, the first witness was the child's aunt Ellen Simmons, who told the Coroner that she was in service at Windsor. She stated that the deceased was the child of her sister, but that she was abroad at the moment. The witness said that because of that, she herself had occasionally visited the child at Eastlake Road. She said that her sister had looked after the child until the previous September when it began to walk. Her sister had managed to make a basic living as a dressmaker, but when she was offered the post of lady's maid travelling abroad with her mistress, she looked for someone to care for the child. Miss Simmons had seen an advertisement in the local newspaper and had told her sister who offered to pay 6s a week to Reeves for the baby's keep and all his clothing. The witness told the jury that she and her sister had taken the child to Reeve's house in September 1890.

Miss Simmons told the Coroner that her sister went abroad in the second week in November, and admitted that the rich woman that her sister worked for, had no idea that her travelling companion had a child in London. She had seen her nephew on 16 December and noted that he was in a poorly state. The witness had received a note from Reeves saying to come at once that the child was very ill, and the prisoner had told her that he had severe diarrhoea brought on by teething. When Miss Simmons asked where the child was, Reeves told her that he was in the front room on the ground floor. She paid her the money that her sister owed her, and also gave her 2s for postage stamps. On the following day Miss Simmons received a note stating that Reeves had paid for a doctor to come and see little Stephen, and the child was 'a little better, but required expensive treatment'. Miss Simmons obligingly sent her £1.15s. The witness described how she had seen the child again on 27 December and he appeared a little better, but she admitted that she stayed no more than 15 minutes. Miss Simmons told the inquest that she sent another £1 for doctors treatment again, after she received a letter on 30 December. On 3 January she went to the house, but by then Stephen had been moved to the NSPCC shelter. On being told this, the witness went to the shelter and saw him there same day, and was appalled at his condition. After his death she later identified his body.

Miss Simmons told the Coroner that each time saw Stephen he was in lying in the front parlour of the house, and only on one other occasion did she see another child. She stated that she had just entered the kitchen when Reeves was taking another little girl out of the front room. When Miss Simmons enquired about the child she told her that she was looking after one of her daughter's children. The witness stated that was only other child she had ever seen, and had no idea that Reeves was caring for any more children, or that she was a baby farmer. The witness told the Coroner that when her nephew had gone to Alice Reeves he was a strong healthy child, who had never had a days illness in his short life. Dr Patrick George Simpson of Coldharbour Lane, Camberwell stated that he was called in to see the deceased child, Stephen on December 10 when he visited Eastlake Road, after being summoned there by Reeves. The woman had told him that her husband was a sailor in the navy and had just sailed from Plymouth. She intimated that the boy was her own child, and that she also had a 3 year old and another infant, that all had been delicate from birth. Dr Simpson reported that Reeves was holding the child, Stephen in her arms, but he was in such a dirty condition, that the doctor told her to clean him up and he would call back the next day. The following day Dr Simpson returned and found the child a lot cleaner, but still in a very emaciated state. He asked her why the child looked so ill and starved, and she told him that she had been away from home for a month, and that in her absence the baby had been looked after by her daughter. She claimed that she had returned home when her daughter telegraphed her to say that the child was ill. Dr Simpson said that the house was in a filthy state and the air was most offensive. He went again on Monday 13 December and noted that Stephen was worse again and as dirty as he had been previously. Upon further inspection he noted that the infant was in a dying condition. He had told her that the child was in imminent danger, and that he needed to be removed instantly to a hospital. He gave Reeves a letter requesting that the child be admitted to St Thomas's hospital, but the following day the letter was returned to him unopened. A note was attached, stating that Reeve's mother would not allow the baby to be taken to the hospital.

On his next visit on Saturday 15 December, Dr Simpson told her that in that case of the child Stephen, he would not be held responsible any further. However Reeves asked him to look at another child, who she told him was her daughters. She claimed that her daughter was a widow with five children, who had come back to live with her. He noted another four children at the house, and once again Reeves told him that they all had diarrhoea. She brought little Nellie into the room and asked him to prescribe for her, which he did. He spoke strongly to her to keep the children clean, and the prisoner said she was doing her best for them. He told the Coroner that on one occasion he had ordered milk for a baby, but later found that Reeves had thickened it with gruel, and he had told her off about it. He informed the prisoner he would come back on the 18 December but could not get into the house, although he could hear people moving about inside. He went back the following day on December 19 and saw Stephen and the prisoner, with baby of two or three months in her arms, that she said was her daughter's child. Dr Simpson stated that whilst they had been at the NSPCC shelter, a special nurse had been employed to look after the two seriously ill children, Stephen Simmons and Louise Mary Reeves. Continuing with his evidence Dr Simpson said that he was told that Stephen had died on 9 January and he attended the post mortem, which was being undertaken by Dr Pepper and Mr Gabe. They found that pneumonia was the cause of death, accelerated by neglect and cold. Professor Augustus John Pepper of St Mary's hospital told the inquest that he had undertaken the post mortem. He too testified as to the wasted condition of the body, and agreed with the statement of his colleague on the cause of death. One of the jury asked if the lives of any of the children had been insured, but Inspector Patton stated that he had been unable to find out any information about that. The jury returned a verdict of manslaughter against Alice Reeves, and she was ordered on the Coroners warrant to take he trial at the Old Bailey.

On Thursday 16 January 1891 Reeves was informed that another child, Louise Mary Reeves had died, and the following morning the prisoner was brought before the magistrates at Lambeth Police Court. Inspector Patton stated that it was thought that the death of another child, Lewis Reeves was imminent, and the prisoner was now charged with manslaughter. Surgeon Mr John R Gabe described the children in the shelter as all in a very weak condition. After all the evidence was heard, Reeves asked to account for the state of the children, and she claimed that some of them were so emaciated because they had been suffering from teething problems. Dr Reid was recalled and asked whether teething would cause the emaciation which had been found in the children, to which he replied 'certainly not'. Inspector Patton told the magistrate 'that was as far as he could go today', and Reeves was again remanded for a week. However the next day she was in court again, charged with two more deaths. Albert Reeves aged 16 months had died the previous Friday and Lewis Reeves who had died that morning.

On Tuesday January 21 an inquest was held on the bodies of the two children at the Holborn Town Hall. The case of Lewis Reeves was heard first, and a curious story was revealed. It was now certain that Lewis's proper name was Lewis de Clair. James Spencer Atkinson, a solicitor told the inquest that a couple had asked Reeves to adopt their baby Lewis in October of 1890 for the sum of £20, and Reeves had agreed. An arrangement to visit the house with the child was arranged for 13 October. Reeves appeared to be surprised to see the solicitor attending with the couple. They said that their name was 'de Clair' and the mother was obviously French. The father of the child told her that the baby had been placed with a neglectful nurse, and that explained why he was in such a poor condition. Reeves began to spin them a tale, telling them that she was the wife of Henry Reeves, a successful architect and that she had always loved children. For many years she had cared for her sister's children, but her sister was now going abroad, and therefore she had decided to adopt a child of her own. Incredibly the couple thought that the conditions of the house appeared suitable, and an agreement was reached. It was decided that the mother would visit the child four times a year, but what Reeves did not know was that a short while afterwards, both parents were dead and the child had been left an orphan. Inspector Patton whilst at the house, had looked at the other children and noted that Lewis was better fed than the others. Reeves had told him that she had fed Lewis on tapioca, beef tea, rolled oatmeal and sometimes biscuits. However Inspector Patton noted that even though the child was not in such an emaciated state as the others, nevertheless had been 'moaning and groaning'. Lewis had been removed to the shelter with the others, but there he had contracted measles and died. Dr Pepper stated that he had completed a post mortem, and found the child had weighed less than 14½ lbs.

Inspector Patton gave evidence that he was employed by NSPCC and described how he had gone to the house with Sgt Cockerell. He saw eight children and was told by Reeves that Lewis was only 12 months old, instead of being in fact aged 20 months. The prisoner said 'I ask for justice. The gentleman is speaking false. My life is in danger. I must speak'. Mr Biron simply told her to be quiet. Other witnesses confirmed the evidence already given at the magistrates court and the inquests. No witnesses were called in Reeves defence, although she made a long and rambling statement to the effect that certain witnesses, who would have spoken in her defence, had not been called. The prisoner claimed that she had always done her best for the children and had endeavored to get the best medical help that she could afford. The magistrate Mr Biron stated that from the evidence it seemed that the prisoner had not done everything in her power to save the child, and the evidence was confusing in the extreme. However he thought that it failed to show willful neglect, and he urged the jury to come to the conclusion that the child died from natural causes. The jury accordingly brought in a verdict of 'natural causes' for Lewis. The Coroner told the inquest that he would now look into the case for Albert Reeves. Surgeon Mr Gabe gave evidence that when the child was brought into the shelter, he was exceedingly emaciated and feeble. He could find no cause for its condition, apart from the fact that he had been systematically starved. The child had began to improve with better treatment, but because it was so feeble he had doubts that it would recover. So he was not surprised to be told that the child had died, and he gave the cause of death as 'starvation'. Dr Pepper also gave evidence that when the child arrived at the shelter he weighed 13½ lbs when he should have weighed around 22 lbs.

Reeves was brought into Lambeth police court on 30 January 1891 where further evidence was heard from the police. It was revealed in court that Reeves had received twelve children in the last six months, and of these, at least four had died. The police revealed that she had even lied about the death of one of the children, in order that the mother might continue to pay the money each week. The court was told that Reeves had received a letter from a married woman called Mrs Caroline Major, who was living apart from her husband. Mrs Major had answered an advertisement in the weekly newspaper and asked Reeves if she would care for her child Alice. As a result of these negotiations the mother took her little girl to the house on Eastlake Road. It was agreed that she would pay Reeves 5s a week for the upkeep of the child. On 2 January Mrs Major had received a telegram from Reeves, and when she went to the house she told the mother that a charge of baby farming had been made against her. She implored Mrs Major to say that she had not paid her money, but that she looked after the child in return for some washing. Reeves stated that two children had been left with her by people who gave false names and addresses, and she had not been paid for them either. At this point Inspector Patton stated that he did not propose to go any further that day and asked for another remand, and the magistrate Mr Biron agreed. The prisoner handed the magistrate a hand written defence statement, and he told her that he would read it carefully. Reeves told him that on the following week she was intending to bring a witness, a doctor who would speak on her behalf. Mr Biron stated that she should be given every facility to bring some kind of evidence on her own behalf.

The next week, when the court reconvened, Reeves called Dr Cahill, an assistant doctor to Dr Burke of Camberwell, into the court. He stated that he had been called out to see Stephen Simmons, but he failed to find any organic disease. He stated that the child was clean and had clean clothing, but when pressed he admitted that it was so emaciated, that he thought it probable that his life was in danger. The Coroner asked him if he had said as much to Reeves, but he told him that he had said nothing at the time, and she had paid him 10s. The daughter of the prisoner, also called Alice Reeves stated that she had never lived at Eastlake Road with her mother, and was now living with friends and she begged that the address would not be made public. She told the Coroner that she had stayed a week with her mother at Christmas, and during that time the children were bathed every day, and fed well on bread and milk, tapioca and rice and some had raw beef juice, brandy and eggs. She claimed that every care had been given to the children whilst she had been there. Surgeon Mr Gabe was recalled and asked his opinion of children of such a young age being fed on such food, and he answered that 'it would be most improper to give a child, eggs, brandy or the raw juice of meat, as such food would be injurious to any child's health'. Reeves also brought receipts for the amount of milk she had purchased whilst the children were in her care, which were produced and shown to the jury. After more than an hour's consultation however, the jury found her guilty of causing the deaths of Lewis and Albert Reeves and she was committed to take her trial at the Old Bailey at the next assizes.

On Saturday 7 February 1891 Charles Stanley May, a solicitors clerk aged 51 was charged for being concerned with his wife in neglecting several children 'whereby their lives had been in great danger'. Inspector Patton stated that when he went to arrest Mr May he asked to be tried with his wife. As a consequence he wished only on this occasion to bring forward some general information as to the condition of the children, and to establish the fact that May had been in the house, and had witnessed their neglect. The magistrate Mr Biron stated that he must prove that May knew the children were in the house, and Inspector Patton agreed. He repeated the evidence that on the night he had arrested Reeves, he had found May sitting in an armchair in the kitchen. When the inspector asked him who he was, May had told him that he was a lodger. The magistrate's clerk Mr Nixon, read out a statement which had been received from the prisoner's son William May, stating that his father had assisted in the care of the children. Police Sergeant Cooper stated that at 7.30 pm the previous night, he had gone to the house on Eastlake Road and found the prisoner. He told him that he was arresting him with the neglect of children and May had told him that he was innocent, and again claimed that he was only a lodger at the house. Nevertheless he was arrested and taken to the police station where the warrant was read out to him. He denied having any care of the children and had never been authorized by any person to take care of them. His solicitor Mr Moss submitted that there was no evidence against his client, who had been for some time in a very bad state of health. Consequently he hoped that May could have bail if the matter was to be pursued. The magistrate agreed and he was bailed on a sum of £25 to take his trial with his wife.

Four days later on Wednesday 11 February 1891 Alice Reeves was brought to the Old Bailey. Mr Justice Charles stated that the case should stand over to the next sessions, in order that the evidence could be heard which would result in the husband being tried alongside his wife. Therefore it was on Monday 17 March 1891 before the two prisoner's were brought before Mr Justice Hawkins, charged with the manslaughter of the two children and for ill treating five other children under their care. Both prisoners pleaded not guilty and were defended by Mr Bourne and Mr Muir. Mr C Mathews and Inspector Patton were instructed to prosecute the case on behalf of the NSPCC. Mr Justice Hawkins heard all the evidence and after summing up the case, he stated that it appeared to him that Alice Reeves had taken in all those children in order to make a profit. Afterwards she had grossly neglected and left them, utterly callously and indifferent to their fate. He told the court:

'if a person entered upon an obligation or contract to take the charge of another, that person was bound to provide the necessaries of life. If during any period of such obligation, a person willfully neglected his or her duty in such a manner as to cause death, that person was guilty of the crime of manslaughter'.

The jury took just a few minutes to find Alice Reeves guilty. Mr Mathews pointed out that there were other offences against the prisoner, but he proposed to offer no evidence against Charles Stanley May, who was then found not guilty and discharged. Reeves was told that her sentence was to be deferred and she left the dock. The following day Reeves was returned back into court where she was given a ten year prison sentence.

Chapter Twelve: Mary Boyle

This baby farmer had been in the business a long time and was well practiced in the arts of lying, by telling anxious mothers what they wanted to hear. Indeed she became so plausible that she took dangerous risks to achieve her own ends. Like many others of her kind she was adept at covering her tracks and evading the police authorities. However the one thing which makes her different from the rest, was the way in which, sometimes within hours of receiving the child, she would callously abandon it. No doubt by using such a passive method, she hope not only evade capture, to also to absolve herself from blame if the child died.

In 1881 Mary Boyle was fifteen years of age when she first came to the notice of the police, when she was already exploiting children. Her parents had always found her to be difficult to manage, and she was in the habit of staying away from home for days and nights on end. Boyle came to the police's attention after being told that she would call on neighbour's and offer to take their child or children for a walk. When they returned without boots or wearing apparel, the mothers started to complain. Boyle was also accused of stopping children in the streets and taking money from them. About this time she had obtained a position as a nurse to a family, but was soon dismissed due to her brutal treatment of the children in her care. But it was alleged to be three years later before she started in her position as a baby farmer, by adopting children for money and then swiftly abandoning them. Like many before her, it was thought that in her lifetime hundreds of children had been through her hands. In one case, the mother was unable to pay much towards the upkeep of her child. Boyle, eying the expensive baby clothes which the mother had brought to give to the new adoptive parents, told her that she would take the child for the bag of clothes alone, to which the desperate mother agreed. About three weeks later a constable on night duty on Clapham Common, discovered the child alive and fully dressed, lying by a seat near to one of the ponds. The child was taken to the infirmary where sadly it later died.

By the time Mary Boyle was 24 she was living on Windsor Street, City Road, London when she was brought before the Worship Street magistrates, charged with abandoning a female child on 5 June 1890 that was only 14 days old. The baby had been left in the doorway of a block of flats called Chichester Buildings in Shoreditch. The police were alerted and one of the lodgers in the house recalled speaking to Mary Boyle. Half an hour later the baby was found abandoned. Boyle was brought into court and confronted with the mother, who told them that the little girl was illegitimate and she had been born on 11 May 1890. On May 18 she had inserted an advertisement in a weekly newspaper imploring some kind person 'to adopt a pretty fair baby girl for love'. Unfortunately Boyle answered the letter purporting to be a woman called Mrs Witherington who had just lost her own child, and wished to adopt another to replace it. She told the anxious mother that if the infant was entrusted to her, she would treat it with much care and tenderness. On 29 May the mother handed over the child at Waterloo Station. The Medical Officer for the Shoreditch workhouse, Mr Reason told the magistrates that it had been raining on the night the child had been abandoned, and she was suffering from convulsions. He said that the baby was taken to the workhouse where she was examined, and he found signs of starvation. The baby only weighed 4 lbs 15 ounces, when it should have weighed at least 12 or 12½ lbs. Sadly the child died three days later. A former landlady, Mrs Mills attended the court and told the magistrates that the prisoner had taken a room in her house on 30 May 1890 and when she moved in she had a young baby with her. A few days later the baby had gone and when Mrs Mills was asked where the baby was, Boyle replied that she had left it in the charge of 'some people'. Soon after that she had moved out owing rent. The magistrate sentenced Mary Boyle to 12 months imprisonment with hard labour.

It was later reported in the local newspapers of the time that Boyle had been married and had been living with her husband in the beginning of 1893, but following him being sent to prison for his ill-treatment of her in February, she had taken furnished lodgings in Olney Street, Walworth. True to form she had not been in lodgings long before her landlady found her with a baby, which she claimed was her own. The landlady became suspicious when two days later the baby had gone. Around 4 March a baby had been found by a woman working at a farm in Maidstone. The woman was walking along a secluded lane, when she heard a cry and to her astonishment found a baby. It was lying in some thick woods, near a ditch and was placed about five feet from the roadway. The child was dressed in expensive clothes all monogrammed with a red 'J' on them, and looked to be no more than four to six weeks old. The woman picked up the child and took it to Maidstone Workhouse, where one of the relieving officers placed an advert in the local newspapers giving a description of the child and its clothing. No information as to its identity was ever given, and the child remained in the workhouse. Only much later was similar clothing found to be at the house of Mary Boyle. Police enquiries had established that a boy who passed earlier down the same lane, saw a woman carrying a baby and then later saw her without the child. On another occasion when she returned back to her lodgings and the landlady asked her where the baby was, and she told her that she didn't want her husband to know about the child, so she had 'put it away' where it will be looked after. A few days later the same landlady saw that the body of a child had been found floating in the Grand Surrey Canal, and when she drew Boyle's attention to it she remarking 'what a hard hearted wretch anyone must be, who could kill a poor little baby'. Boyle's reply was not recorded.

On the 24 March Boyle went to the stationer's shop where she had made arrangements to receive letters addressed to the names of Mrs Green, Campbell and Kemp. At the time she was carrying two babies in her arms, which she told the woman serving in the shop were her sister's children. Boyle said that she was caring for them whilst her sister saw her sailor husband off to sea. An hour later she was seen leaving the Elephant and Castle Railway Station without any children, and what became of them was never discovered. Boyle also left an infant at a charitable institution in Bermondsey where she told them that she would return later to collect it. Needless to say she did not return and the child, who was thought to be delicate, was taken to the workhouse where it died a few days later. The very same evening Boyle was seen returning to her lodgings once more, with yet another child which was remarkably well dressed. Once again she told her landlady that it was her sister's baby, but that child too disappeared and its whereabouts was never known. At that time Mary Boyle was 27 years of age and it was reported that she had now carried on the profession of baby farmer for many years. The walls of the room in which Boyle lived, was covered with religious tracts, which she told her landlady she committed one to memory every day. Later that same month another baby was found in Boyle's room, dead, which she claimed had been her own and that it had fallen from the bed onto the floor. An inquest was held and a verdict of death from natural causes had been given. It was only later established that this child had belonged to a woman called Miss White, a servant who had her child adopted by Boyle for £3. However Boyles career as a baby farmer was about to come to an end.

A letter which had been found in her room was from a young governess called Miss Mabel Louisa Reed. She was aged 23 and unmarried when she gave birth to a male child in March 1893. On 29 April she answered an advertisement to adopt a child from Boyle, who on this occasion was calling herself Mrs Green. The letter stated that her husband was a wealthy tea merchant at Eastbourne, and she had given birth to a dead baby seven weeks earlier. She said that she wanted the child in order that friends would think it was her own. She told Miss Reed that she would like to call it Arthur after her husband, and when the boy became of age he would have a share in the tea company. Boyle concluded the letter:

'we should dearly love to adopt your little darling entirely as our own, and have it registered in our own name. It would have the most loving care, a good Christian home, and every care and attention'.

A week later Mary Boyle went to meet Miss Reed and her male child aged six weeks at London Bridge Station. Miss Reed reluctantly gave her the little boy and the £3 required premium. Boyle gave her a receipt and told her that she was going to Gravesend to meet some friends. Miss Reed told her that she wished to see her son every week, to which Boyle agreed. When Miss Reed got home however she noted that the receipt had no address on it, and became concerned. However as she was due to see the woman and her child again, she put her worries on one side. The very first day that Miss Reed had arranged to meet her son was Friday 6 May 1893 at the London Bridge Station, but although she waited for many hours it was in vain. Miss Reed met every train from Eastbourne, but there was no sign of Boyle or her son. She then went to Kennington Road police station to ask the advise of the police and spoke to Detective Inspector Harvey. When she gave a description of the woman who had taken her baby, the inspector realised that it fitted that of Mary Boyle who was already known to the police as a baby farmer.

The following day there was a knocking at the door of her house on Olney Street, Walworth and when Boyle opened it, she found Detective Sergeant Chide and Detective Burgess. They told her that she had been accused of stealing a child who belonged to a woman called Miss Reed. The house was searched and although there was no child at the house and Boyle strongly denied it, she was taken into custody. Boyle was placed in a line up amongst other women, where she was quickly identified by Miss Reed. When DI Harvey arrested her on the charge of stealing the child, she stated 'I did not steal it. How can you call it stealing when it was given to me to adopt'. Harvey then asked her where the baby was and she told him 'I will not tell you if you keep me here for 25 years'. He again asked her where it was, and Boyle told him that it with a ministers family at Leicester, and assured him that the baby would be well looked after. Mary Boyle was brought into the Lambeth Police Court on Monday 8 May where she sobbed loudly. A chair was found for her so that she might be allowed to sit during the examination. Detective Inspector Harvey gave an outline of the charges against her, of stealing the child and fraudulently taking £3 from Miss Mabel Reed by trickery. He also told the court that the prisoner had other children in her care, and there had been an inquest on one of them only a few weeks previously. The magistrate, Mr Hopkins asked him if the child belonging to Miss Reed had been found, but DI Harvey was forced to confess that it hadn't.

Mr Sims who was prosecuting the case on behalf of the Treasury, stated that it had been reported to the Director of Public Prosecutions. He had been told that Boyle had been carrying on the business of baby farming for many years, and had previously served a prison sentence of 12 months for a similar offence. Mr Sims stated that he had evidence of at least two other similar offences which he would place before the court, although those children too had been unaccounted for. One of the magistrates, Mr Hopkins granted a remand and told the prisoner that 'she stood in a very serious position'. Thankfully later that day the missing child of Miss Reed's was found in Gravesend, lying in a ditch on a lonely road. The child had been crying due to the close proximity of some stinging nettles. He was taken to Hastings Workhouse where he was later identified by his mother, and it was said that despite its uncomfortable position, the baby appeared to be none the worse for its exposure. Thankfully on this occasion Miss Reed was allowed to take her child home. At the next appearance on Tuesday 16 May 1893 the prisoner was brought back into court. Miss Reed appeared again and she told the court about her dealings with the prisoner. A man called Edward T White then gave evidence about finding the baby at Gravesend. He said that he had been walking along French Lane accompanied by a young woman, when they both heard a baby cry on the other side of the hedge. When he went into the field, he saw the baby dressed in white, lying at the foot of a tree. The baby wore a little cape which had been pulled over its face, and it was crying. He took the child to the Gravesend police station. The young woman he was with, Miss M A Bowen confirmed his story, adding that just before they heard the child cry, she saw a woman, who she now recognised as Boyle walking along French Lane.

The servant in the stationers shop called Mary Pierce told the court that the prisoner had received many letter addressed to various names, and that sometimes she had as many as twenty letters in a day. She told the court that on one particular day a letter was addressed to the prisoner which had a crest on the back, and had a post mark from the West End of London. Mary Boyle told Pierce:

'Ah this ought to bring me a slice of luck. I ought to make a few quid out of a job like this. There is one thing I like about these West End people; they don't worry you much after you take their baby'

Soon after this encounter, Boyle told the servant that she did not want to use the stationers shop to receive any more letters. After hearing Pierce's evidence the prisoner was remanded for another week, and she was hissed at as she left the dock.

Meanwhile further enquiries were made by the Kent police, now acting under instructions from Scotland Yard. Newspapers were asked to give publicity to the following alias's under which the prisoner had passed, and for anyone with any information to get in touch with them. The names which Boyle had used were Mrs Vaughan, Ellis, Green, Boys, Camp, Campbell, Sophia Smith, Roberts or Mrs Mary Wilson. During their investigations they had elicited many stories of young women handing over their babies to the prisoner. It was quickly established that during the last five months, many young children and infants had been found in isolated areas about the Maidstone district. During the time that Boyle was imprisoned, more and more letters were sent to the Kent police, from young women at various addresses who had handed their child over to her. When Boyle was informed in her cell that several other similar charges were to be made against her, she became frightened. Boyle claimed to have become so ill that the prison surgeon Dr Gilbert had ordered her removal to the prison infirmary. Meanwhile more and more cases were coming to the attention of the police authorities. A woman named Mason told the police that she had given birth to a male child on February 9 1893 and advertised it as being ready for adoption on February 26. Two days later she received a reply from a woman signing herself as Mrs Green. Mason later met the woman and the child was handed over along with £2, only days later did she hear that the baby had been abandoned in Maidstone. She identified Mary Boyle as the woman who had taken her baby. Two other young servant girls named Kent and White also gave evidence against Boyle, stating that they had paid her £2 and £3 for her to adopt their babies. A Detective Sergeant Chick told the court that on 16 May, when he was escorting the prisoner back to her cell, she asked him if any more babies had been found. He told her that they were interviewing mothers, and when she asked their names and was told Kent and White, she told him 'those two babies are dead'. Thankfully on this occasion, she was wrong regarding one of the children. It was later established on the 30 May that the Kent child was in Greenwich Workhouse.

The following week on Tuesday 23 May, Mary Boyle was brought into court again at Lambeth, and it was noted that the court was crowded with young women. Several witnesses gave testimony about handing their babies over to the prisoner. They all told the same story, that she had fabricated her own personal circumstances, always making out that she was a respectable, married woman. When one of the witnesses described how she had queried, why Boyle wanted money when her husband had such a respectable position of tea merchant, church minister or deacon, she told her that she 'just wanted the money to buy a few things for the little one'. In all cases, although she had told the poor mother that she would write to her, they never saw or heard from her again. Once again she was hissed as she left the court room. It was reported that by the time she was in court again on Tuesday 6 June, five more charges had been brought against her, and numerous other charges were still being investigated. Several other people gave evidence of seeing Boyle with a baby and later without it. One landlady gave evidence that when Boyle came to her lodgings in a street off the Old Kent Road she had a child with her. The landlady politely enquired whose the child was and in reply Boyle said:

'Oh I cannot understand some people. They want to know so much about other peoples business, but I don't mind telling you. My sister's husband is a captain, and whilst he has been away she has had a child, which I am sorry to say does not belong to him. I am minding it for a day or so for her until he goes to sea again. If anyone should say anything to you about the baby, you say its mine and I am going to put it out to nurse'.

As an illustration of how devious Mary Boyle could be, the court heard that two days later she walked into Bermondsey Police Station and asked to see the Inspector on duty. She told him some concocted story about being left with a male baby from an acquaintance who had asked her to look after it whilst she went for a job at a local chocolate factory. Boyle claimed the woman had spoken to her at noon and stated that she would meet her in a certain public house. She had waited for four hours and the woman had not returned, and she asked the Inspector what she was supposed to do. He took her name and address and directed a constable to take her the workhouse where the child was left. On the way there she told the constable 'I cannot understand a mother being so cruel as to leave her dear little boy in the hands of a stranger, and then to go away and abandon it to the world'. When she got back to her lodgings she told the landlady that 'I have put the baby out to nurse, but it nearly broke my heart to part with the little duck. I thank God however, it would be well looked after'.

Another instance of her deviousness was given in court when the magistrates were told that on 14 March 1893 Boyle had gone to St John's Nursery, Bedford Street, Walworth and enquired if they could take care of her 'dear little Arthur' the following day. Boyle gave the excuse that she had a situation which would take up the whole of the day, and appeared surprised at the smallness of the charge. The nurse offered to show her around the nursery, and she expressed delight at the care and thought that had been expended on the provision for the children. That same night Boyle picked up another child she had adopted for £4 which she conveyed to the nursery on the following morning, as arranged. Needless to say she was never seen again, nor was any trace of her found at the address she had given. Sadly 'dear little Arthur' had to be sent to Bermondsey Workhouse, where he became ill and died a few weeks later. In both these cases Boyle had been identified although no trace of the mothers had been found. The magistrates listened to other evidence of witnesses finding babies hidden away, before she was found guilty and sent to take her trial at the assizes.

On Friday 15 July 1893 at Maidstone Assizes Mary Boyle was indicted of 10 separate counts of stealing, or obtaining by fraud, a number of children who she afterwards abandoned. She was undefended and the prosecution was undertaken by Mr Gye. DS Chick told the assizes that she had been turned out of her lodgings on New Kent Road in 1890 as a consequence of her ill-treatment of two children that had been in her care. She had stated that one child was her own and the other was her sister's. The judge asked the Sergeant what had become of those children and he told his lordship that they had never been traced. DS Chick referred to her 12 months prison sentence in 1890 for abandoning a child, and stated that at least four other children which she was known to have had in her possession could not be traced. After all the women gave their evidence about the handing over of their children, the prosecution brought their case to a close. When Boyle was asked to present her own defence, she told the judge that all the children had been handed over to a Mrs Green who had promised to look after them. The jury found her guilty, and she sobbed bitterly as the judge told her that it was one of the worst cases he had before him for some time. He stated that:

'you seem to have been at the business for a long while, and that at least three of the children that had been in your care have never been traced. Whether you had killed them or made away with them, I do not know but I hope that they were being comfortably cared for. It would probably never be known however, unless you chose to speak. No one could say whether the children had been made away with, or had died from your cruelty and neglect'

Boyle was still sobbing when he ordered that she serve a maximum penalty of 14 years in prison.

Even after the assizes had ended the reports continued about this terrible woman. It was reported that since December of 1872 Detectives Inspector Harvey and Detectives Chick and Burgess had estimated that hundreds of children had passed through her hands, but they had only succeeded in tracking ten of the children that had been in Boyles care. Of these only five could be accounted for, and that two of the remaining five had been found abandoned in Gravesend. On another occasion, Boyle had been seen leaving London Bridge with a child in her arms, and an hour later she returned without it. A porter employed at Gravesend later discovered the body of a baby tied up in an old petticoat and lying in a ditch. It was thought that the child had been thrown from a passing train. Such callousness could not be understood by many people, who were desperate to understand Boyles motives. Today we have more understanding of people with little empathy towards their victims. The investigations into the murders committed by Amelia Dyer suggest that killing babies gave her an almost God-like power. After each child had died she found peace within herself, after she had disposed of the latest little body. It has also been suggested that she would have derived some maternal pleasure from looking at them lying at peace. It is possible that Boyle understood the same kind of feelings. After she had been tried, the newspapers seemed unable to believe that she had made:

'the most lying statements in order to obtain a child, with no other object in view or advantage other than to secure it for a paltry sum, before abandoning it in a most reckless and uncaring manner'.

It would be a long time indeed before the crimes of baby farmer Mary Boyle was forgotten.

Chapter Thirteen: Ada Chard Williams

This baby farmer is the last one of only three women in this book who were hanged for their crimes, and like the others there is no information about why she took up that murderous career or how many children she actually killed. In 1899 Ada Chard Williams was very pleased with her life. She was 24 years of age and had been married for seven years to a man who was older than she was. She was a good looking woman with fair hair and quite tall at 5 foot 7 inches. Her husband William was aged 41 and said to have gained a Master's Degree from Balliol College. He appeared to be very well connected and was somewhat smaller than his wife, at 5 feet 1 inch. The couple had met through an advertisement in the matrimonial section of a newspaper, and they had got on so well together that they married a short time later. Williams herself was the daughter of a fairly successful farmer named Robert Street of Horsham in Sussex and had been brought up very respectfully.

Williams's life was about to be blown apart on 27 September 1899 when the body of a little girl was found on the foreshore of the River Thames, covered with a sack. The body had been found by William Stokes, a waterman at Church Dock, Battersea about 9 am. He saw a brown paper parcel tied up with string, and noted to his horror a child's foot sticking out of it. He managed to drag the parcel out of the water, and gave it to Police Constable David Voice, who took it to a mortuary at Battersea. Opening the parcel PC Voice looked inside and found some pink coloured flannelette material wrapped tightly around the body of a child. Its head and face was in a linen bag, which was tied up tightly around the neck with string. The legs had been bound in strong cord and tied up in a fetal position, in order to make the body as small as possible. PC Voice sent for the police surgeon Dr Felix Charles Kempster, who cut the cord around the neck. At this point the police were convinced that a systematic plan of baby farming and murder had been carried out in the area, which would rival that of Amelia Dyer. An inquest was held on the child's body on Monday October 2 1899 by Coroner Mr A Braxton Hicks. Owing to the peculiar circumstances of the case, and the distressing fact that other children had been found murdered under similar conditions, the enquiry was held behind closed doors. Dr Kempster told the Coroner that he had undertaken the post mortem on the little body. He thought the child had been in the water since around 23 September. He found a large bruise on the child's skull which he deduced must have been made with some violence, but was not the result of a fall. There was a quantity of clotted blood between the skin and the skull, but there was no fractures. The lungs were congested and the police surgeon thought the child had been suffocated or strangled. Dr Kempster gave his opinion that it would only take between 60 to 90 seconds to suffocate a child in that way. He estimated that the child had been stunned before being strangled, with what appeared to be a sash cord from a window. After the initial details had been heard, the inquest was adjourned for a month for the police to continue with their enquiries.

When details about the child which had been found were published, the mother, Miss Florence Jones aged just 20 years visited the Battersea mortuary. There she identified her child as one she had given birth to on December 17 1897 at Clapham. The child's name was Selina Ellen Jones. Miss Jones told the police that her child had been a beautiful blond haired baby girl aged 21 months. Since Miss Jones had to work, the child had been placed with two other woman for which she paid 5s a week, and had visited the child several times. In July the child's father ceased to pay any more maintenance, and Miss Jones felt that she had no option but to have the little girl adopted. She saw an advert in *Woolwich Herald* on August 18 1899 from a couple wanting to adopt a child. The advert stated:

'A young married couple would adopt a healthy baby; every care and comfort; good references given; very small premium. Write first to Mrs Hewetson, 4 Bradmore Lane. Hammersmith.'

In response Miss Jones received a reply stating that the couple wanted a premium of £5 and included an address at The Grove, Hackney. Miss Jones responded, and also enclosing a photograph of the little girl, which had been taken when she was about 9 months old. Miss Jones and Mrs Hewetson agreed to meet at Woolwich Station on Thursday 31 August, and from there they went to Miss Jones' mothers house. She introduced Mrs Hewetson to her mother, who told her that they only wanted the child to be adopted for a short while and then have her back again, to which Mrs Hewetson agreed. Miss Jones told the woman that she wanted to see the baby every fortnight, and her mother stated her intention to visit Mrs Hewetson too. They then made an agreement to hand over the baby at Charing Cross Station the following Thursday. Just before the arranged date Miss Jones received a letter, signed 'May Hewetson' which stated:

'I hope you will try and bring as many of the little ones things as you possibly can, as my husbands mother is coming over from Scotland one day next week, and intends staying a fortnight. So I want to make baby as pretty and dainty as I possibly can, because I shall want the old lady to take a fancy to her. It may be to her future benefit'.

Miss Jones handed over her little girl and £3 of the £5 premium. The following week she was expecting to see her daughter again, where she had agreed to hand over the remaining £2. A short time afterwards, Miss Jones received a letter from the woman saying that they had taken a house in Hammersmith 'so that all the neighbour's would think that the child was their own' and she would write again giving the new address. The following week Miss Jones did not get a letter, and went to the house at The Grove, Hackney where she found another couple installed, who claimed they did not know the former tenant. She went to the address where she had sent the response to the advertisement at 4 Bradmore Lane, and found it was a newspaper shop. On September 4 Miss Jones went to the West London Police Station to make a complaint, and the next thing she knew was a message from the police on 3 October 1899 asking her to go to the Battersea mortuary. She went there and saw the body of her dead child. She was also shown a quantity of clothes which she identified as belonging to her baby, which she had handed over to Mrs Hewetson on August 31.

Miss Jones gave such a detailed description of the woman, that the police knew immediately who this particular baby farmer was. It was reported on the following day the officers of the CID had gone to the house rented by the Williams and found the couple had departed owing rent. A warrant was issued for their arrest and the newspapers were asked for their help in tracing the couple called Mr and Mrs Chard Williams who were wanted on suspicion of murdering the child. The man was described as being:

'aged 40 years, height 5 feet 1 inch, complexion very dark, freckled on the face and hands, skin loose and flabby (especially on the cheeks) small dark grey eyes, eyebrows and short hair with a dark mustache, no whiskers, but a few grey hair above temples, small nose and feet. He is of proportionate build and speaks with a low effeminate voice and is slightly knock-kneed. He might be wearing a pepper and salt jacket, or a black suit and a silk hat, but he always carries a walking stick. He has the appearance of a foreigner. The woman is aged about 28 years, height 5 feet 7 inches, slim build, hair golden and curly or wavy, long features, large mouth, with a good set of teeth. The last time she was seen, she was wearing a black alpaca skirt, white blouse, a black jacket, white straw sailor hat with a black band and black shoes'

The description suggested that they were 'adventurers' who took a house with a good address, occupied it for any time from between a fortnight to three months, and then disappeared owing rent. The report concluded that 'any person having them as lodgers, or seeing them in the street, should at once give information to the police'. At the reconvened inquest on 9 October 1899 the medical testimony of Dr F C Kempster the police surgeon for Battersea, stated that the death of the child had been caused by injuries inflicted before death, possibly by being battered on the skull. PC Voice stated that the way in which the string had been knotted around the body, and the way in which the little body had been tied up, had been the same as that found on three other children's bodies which had been recovered. They had all been found murdered in the same area of Barnes over the last few months. The Coroner Mr Braxton Hicks listened to all the evidence before the jury found a verdict of wilful murder against Mr and Mrs Williams, alias Hewetson.

Once the news about the finding of the child's body and the conclusions of the Coroner had been published, the couple disappeared. Needing money, Williams had found herself a temporary low paid job. She had applied to work as a waitress calling herself Mrs Hewetson, in a coffee shop on Gainsborough Road, Hackney. The business had been owned by a couple known as Mr and Mrs Duplane. They were in the process of selling the shop, but took Williams on for a few weeks. She had posed as a widow, and when she was given the job she asked if she could bring her little boy Freddie with her to live in the room above the shop, to which the proprietors had agreed. The boys antecedents were not known, as to whether she had given birth to him or adopted him, but he joined her in the flat. Williams started the job in late November, and found that the customers were mainly made up of navvies, car men and bricklayers. Mr Duplane meanwhile had sold the business, and on Saturday 11 December they were due to move out of the premises. He had given Williams notice, and she was due to leave on the same day. Williams had told the Duplane's that she lived on her own with the boy, but on December 7 she told them that her brother-in-law had arrived on a visit, and to help her to move out of the premises. He did not stay the night, but appeared back at the shop the following day.

On 5 December 1899 Williams, still using the name Hewetson, sent a letter to the police, which helpfully contained the address on Gainsborough Road, Hackney. It was addressed to:

*The Secretary,
Criminal Investigation Department,
New Scotland Yard.*

Sir, I must apologize taking this liberty, but I see by the papers that I, in conjunction with my husband are suspected of murdering the little female child found at Battersea on September 27 1899. The accusation is positively false. The facts of the case are these. I much against my husbands wish. In August last, advertised for a child, thinking to make a little money. The results of which was the adoption of this little child, with whom I received the sum of £3. My next act was to advertise for a home for a little girl; I used some shop in Warwick Road, West Kensington, I forget the number, but I used the name of Denton or Dalton, I am not sure which. I received about 40 replies, from which I chose one, from George Street or George Road, Croyden. The lady from Croyden, Mrs Smith by name, agreed to take the child for £1 and clothes. I met her at the Falcon Hotel at Clapham Junction about the middle of September. I handed the child over and that was the last I saw of her.'

In the letter Mrs Williams admitted that she had carried on 'a sort of baby farming or adoption service and had five children by this method'. She admitted that two had died in her care, but added that 'I can prove that every attention and kindness was shown to them' while they lived. Williams also claimed that she had tried to find the woman who adopted the little girl, but said that she had destroyed all the letters. She concluded that her husband was not in anyway to blame and had always looked on the matter with the greatest abhorrence, declaring that he would never touched any of the money made in that fashion. In this most extraordinary letter, Williams went on to say that although she was innocent, that many innocent persons had been hanged on similar circumstantial evidence and that she 'did not think it fair, however black the case may look, that the police should act on that kind of evidence'. The letter was signed M HEWETSON. The police had diligently searched for any Mrs Smith on George Road, Croyden, and although one woman named Smith had been identified as living on that same road, she knew nothing about either of the prisoners or the child. Meanwhile, whilst Mr Duplane was making arrangements to move, the police had made arrangement to arrest Ada Chard Williams at the shop on Gainsborough Road.

On the evening of Friday 8 December Detective Inspector James Scott and Detective Joseph Gough, wearing plain clothes visited the coffee shop, where they found Mrs Duplane serving. Detective Gough had disguised himself as a navvy, and wearing big muddy boots, a pair of corduroy trousers and a cap, he went to the counter of the shop and ordered bloaters and bread. In an attempt to get further inside, he went to the room behind the counter to ask how his bloaters were getting on. He then went towards the fire as if to warm himself, and he rubbed his hands together as he complained about the weather. He noted that there was a man in the kitchen who didn't speak and Gough returned back to the counter. When his bloater was served by Mrs Duplane, he asked her where Mrs Hewetson was, and the landlady replied 'Oh I have had enough of her, she is upstairs packing and there is her brother-in-law waiting by the fire to take her away'. As she spoke she indicated the man sitting in the room behind the counter. With this Detective Gough whistled, and at the pre-arranged signal Detective Scott came in dressed in his uniform. He charged the 'brother-in-law' Mr Williams with being concerned in the wilful murder of Selina Ellen Jones the previous September. The man simply answered 'We are guilty of fraud, but innocent of murder'.

Detective Scott then instructed Gough to arrest Mrs Hewetson, who was still packing upstairs. When she asked what it was all about, Gough told her no more details other than he was arresting her on a charge of murder. At this she threw up her hands and almost fainted. When she recovered and went downstairs she said to the two officers 'I know what you have come about its the Battersea job isn't it?' The woman gave her name as Ada Hewetson and her companion gave the name of William Chard Williams. It was clear that that the police had arrested the couple just in time. From their arrangements it seemed that they were on the point of departure, as all their boxes were packed ready for removal to Euston Station. They had intended to travel to Liverpool and after that to go abroad. When Detective Scott examined the trunk that Williams had been packing, he found a large quantity of children's clothes. She told Detective Scott that they had previously lived at The Grove, Hackney. When they arrived at the police station Williams asked the officer 'did you get the letter I sent to Scotland Yard'. When the detective replied in the affirmative, she said 'That is the God's truth. I know it is hard to clear myself, but my husband was not in the house when I took the child away'. By her very words she had incriminated herself in the murder.

The couple were brought into the South Western Police Court on Saturday 9 December 1899 following their arrest, charged with the murder of Selina Ellen Jones. The police surgeon Dr Kempster gave the court details of the post mortem. Inspector Scott said that enquiries were still ongoing and asked for a remand. The magistrate Mr Garrett asked the prisoners if they had anything to say. Williams told him that they were both perfectly innocent of the charge, and despite what she had told Detective Scott, she maintained that the child had been handed over to another woman, claiming it was alive and quite well at the time. It was agreed that they would both be remanded. On Friday 19 January 1900 the couple were again brought back to the South Western Police Court and this time they had a defence counsel Mr F Kent. Dr Kempster was re-called for further examination, and Mr Kent asked him if he adopted a theory that the child was killed by being swung against a wall. He replied 'No, but the theory is a highly probable one'. The prosecution Mr Bodkin told the court about the other dead infants that had been tied up in exactly the same way. The magistrates asked if there was any proof that the other children could be associated with the prisoners, and when told that there wasn't, they agreed that it was therefore not admissible. That concluded the evidence for the prosecution, and when they were asked if they had anything to say, the prisoners repeated that 'we are innocent'. Mr Garrett then committed them to take their trial at the Central Criminal Court.

On Friday 16 February 1900 the couple were brought up at the Old Bailey in front of the judge, Mr Justice Riley. Mr Charles Matthews and Mr Bodkin were the prosecution, and Mr Ernest Wild and Mr McMahon defended both prisoners. It was noted that the prisoners pleaded not guilty, and sat apart in the dock throughout the hearing of the evidence. At no point did they either speak, or in any way try to communicate with each other. They were charged with the death of Selina Ada Jones aged 21 months on September 23 1899. Mr Matthews outlined the case for the jury. A neighbour Mrs Loughborough gave evidence that she had seen two children playing in the garden at The Grove. Chillingly she also stated that she heard both children crying, as if they were being ill treated inside the house later that same evening. She heard Mr Williams call out 'stop that' and his wife shouted back 'hold your noise or I will serve the same to you'. The neighbour also told the court that when the child disappeared at some point around 23 September, Mrs Williams had told her that the mother had come to fetch the little girl away. Miss Florence Jones gave evidence to the circumstances in which she had parted with her baby to the female prisoner. Mr Matthews described how the body of the child had been found, and how the same cord had been found in the prisoners house. At this point the trial was adjourned until the following day.

When the case was resumed on Saturday 17 February the defence Mr Wild stated that he did not intend putting either of the prisoners into the witness box. He warned the jury that 'however much they abhorred the system of baby farming, they should not allow their minds to be so prejudiced or base their judgment upon mere suspicion or innuendo'. Pointing out that the law presumed that prisoners were innocent until proven guilty, and if any doubt existed in the jury's minds, the couple were entitled to an acquittal. Mr Wild claimed that Mrs Williams explanation that she handed the child over to a Mrs Smith was correct. He stated that in the evidence there was a complete absence of motive for the crime. Mr Wild said that:

'the prosecution had not established beyond reasonable doubt the identity of the child, and all this added up to the fact that the prisoner was not a murderess. Her business was merely to sub-farm out the child which she had adopted, for half the sum of money paid to her. Her husband took no part whatsoever in the negotiations or the handing over of the children. It was the duty of the prosecution to prove guilt, and that they had failed to do'.

Mr Matthews then began his summing up, stating that the child had been identified as that of Selina Jones who had been entrusted to Mrs Williams by Miss Jones. All the facts pointed to the conclusion that the child had been brutally murdered by some person or persons unknown. The story told by the woman of handing the child to a 'Mrs Smith' was so suspicious, that it was impossible that the jury will accept it. Mr Mathews claimed that the question of the child's identity had been established 'beyond any reasonable doubt' and it rested with the prisoners to explain satisfactorily, how the child came to be found in the river. He stated that although the female prisoner had claimed that her husband knew nothing of the business of baby farming which she carried out, nevertheless he still lived at the house where the children had been taken for adoption. Mr Mathews submitted that the man had taken a very active part in what his wife did, and the evidence proved both were guilty. If the jury came to the same conclusion therefore, they would have no choice but to convict them both. The judge summed up stating that there was no doubt that this child had been cruelly murdered by some person. If the jury thought that there was a common plan to which both prisoners were party, then they would both be found equally guilty. The child had last been seen alive in their possession, and therefore the only presumption was that they had murdered the child. The jury retired at ten minutes past four, and after half an hour returned back to the courtroom. They told the judge that they had found Mrs William guilty but Mr Williams not guilty, although he had been an accessory after the fact. The sentence of death was passed on her, to which she replied 'thank you my lord' in a very cool manner. The judge and counsel debated the case of Mr Williams as to whether he should be tried as being an accessory after the fact. After a short consultation however, Mr Justice Ridley felt that 'after what had occurred, there could be no useful purpose served in proceeding with a second indictment on Mr Williams'. Mr Matthews stated that no evidence would be offered, and the male prisoner was discharged.

Ada Chard Williams was taken to the condemned cell, where she remained sullen and unspeaking. She was carefully watched by specially trained female staff, to ensure that she did not take her own life prior to the execution. Amelia Dyer unsuccessfully drank two bottles of laudanum the night before she was due to be hung, in the hope of escaping the rope. The large amount she consumed indicated that her body could tolerate it, and that she had been addicted to it for years. It was announced on 20 February 1900 that she would be hanged on Tuesday 6 March at 9 am, but that it will not take place at Newgate, but she would be executed at Wandsworth. Later that same day, she was removed to a cell at Wandsworth prison. Thankfully this was to be a private execution which would be carried out inside the prison, to which members of the public were not admitted. On Saturday March 3 the prison governor of Wandsworth, Colonel Milman was informed that there would be no reprieve and he informed the prisoner. Williams told him that she had not expected there to be. She once again stated that she was innocent, although she was quite resigned to her fate. The same day Mr Williams visited her, as did her mother and brother. On Monday 5 March the hangman James Billington arrived at the prison, accompanied by his son as his assistant at 4 pm. The prisoner had been weighed and the length of drop which was needed was calculated, as was his usual practice. The scaffold and rope had been thoroughly tested, as a precaution against any mishap. That night Williams was moved from her own prison cell into that used by condemned male prisoners, as it was judged to be nearer to the scaffold, and that was where she passed her last night. On the morning of her execution, Williams arose after a restless night at 6 am. She dressed herself in the same dress that she had worn for the trial, and had a light breakfast of bread, butter and tea. The Chaplain remained with her until the last possible moment, but Williams showed no sign of fear at three minutes to nine, when Billington entered the cell and pinioned her arms. She walked calmly to the scaffold without any assistance, and having the white cap placed on her head, the bolt was quickly drawn. So ended the exploits of another cruel and callous baby farmer

The body was left to hang for the usual hour, before being cut down. The Coroners inquest was held at noon, when the jury went to view the body in a plain, deal shell, which was placed across the scaffold. Ada Chard Williams appeared to have died instantaneously, and reporters claimed that her face seemed to be very reposed in death. Apart from a small abrasion under the chin, there was no signs of injury. Colonel Milman stated that the judicial sentence had been carried out satisfactorily. The Coroner asked him if the prisoner had left a confession, and he replied that she hadn't. He added that she was one of the youngest murderers to be hung since private executions were brought in. In reply to another question about Mr Williams, the governor replied that he had described himself as a tutor, but apart from that they knew nothing about him.

Once again, long after her death, the reasons why Ada Chard Williams had become a baby farmer was discussed in the local newspapers. It was assumed that with the kind of education her husband had, he should have been capable of getting a good job and supporting both himself and his wife. But only a few weeks later, the truth came to light, that Williams preferred to live a life of a criminal rather than that of a respectable teacher. Mr William Chard Williams was arrested on a most serious charge of fraud at Surrey Quarter Session since being acquitted of murder. It seems that when he left the courtroom after his acquittal, he was immediately arrested for fraud. Williams was tried on Monday 5 April at Brentford charged with having obtained £8 from Mrs Bliss, a pawnbroker of Twickenham, using false pretences respecting some furniture. It seems that he had gained £40 worth of furniture on hire purchase from Messrs Thomas of Tottenham Court Road, using false references. He only paid £4 and then sold the furniture to Mrs Bliss, declaring that it was his own property. He even produced a forged receipt signed by a Mr Ling, who gave evidence that it was not his signature. Detective Sergeant Moore stated that the prisoner, although he had never been convicted on this crime before, was in the habit of renting houses on a three years tenancy, and furnishing them on the hire purchase system, before disposing of the furniture and paying no rent. He then moved to another house and repeated the process all over again. When the magistrate asked about how he had obtained references from respectable persons of the area, he was told that Williams used addresses of several newspaper shops. When he collected the reference application, he simply completed it himself. William Chard Williams was sentenced to 20 months imprisonment with hard labour.

Chapter Fourteen: Conclusion

The spread of baby farming in the nineteenth century existed because of three basic tenets. The shame for expectant single women, the need to earn a living and the hope that a bastard child could have a better life with a respectable family. Baby farmers hid behind the deaths and abandonment of babies on city streets, the need to make money, and the ease with which a child could be ushered into the next world. These were all factors which led to the wholesale slaughter of children. The Victorian period is well known as one which emphasized family values, so single women who got themselves pregnant had only themselves to blame. In such a world, the baby farmers, known as 'angel makers' flourished. As we have seen the first warning flags which led to the menace of baby farming was the increasing amounts of infanticide, that was occurring in the cities and towns of Britain. The increasing statistics had been ignored for many years, but the problems were longstanding and was not just confined to the Victorian period.

Foundling hospitals had been around since the days of Henry VIII, which had been established to take in and offer hospitality to abandoned and orphaned children, called foundlings. Often these hospitals had baskets or shells at the front door, where desperate women could leave their babies undetected. But many feared that the ease with which mothers could leave their children, would encourage immorality. Although a foundling hospital had been opened in London in 1739, they were generally condemned despite the obvious fact that the need was there. By the nineteenth century the Foundling Hospitals in London, for moral reasons, had changed their admission process. Now it was very different to what it had been in the days of King George II, when babies could be left at the door. Victorian mothers of an illegitimate child, was expected to attend the board of the hospital and formally declare her child to be a bastard. The woman was then expected to give up all rights to the child, and to legally declare that she would not try to claim the child back at a future date. However so rigorous was the admission procedure that in 1825 they admitted only 37 children out of 276 applicants. There is no evidence about what happened to those mothers turned away.

Throughout Britain, the laissez-faire attitude of the Government was slow to make any social changes. In May 1828, even though the numbers of abandoned babies was growing, a decision was made in Parliament that no more money was to be voted for the establishment of yet another foundling hospital. The reason given was because 'such buildings were seen to be extremely mischievous to the public'. By 1840 little had changed. When members of the houses of Parliament became, once again seriously concerned about the victims of infanticide, they discussed the possibility of opening foundling hospitals in every parish in Britain. But this suggestion was again rejected. The same year the *Huddersfield Chronicle* claimed that 'infanticide is growing and spreading in a way that we dare hardly acknowledge even to ourselves'. For those in the front line they could see the danger. In February 1841 the Coroner for Middlesex pleaded for a refuge for illegitimate children to be opened, following the enquiry into yet another death of an infant girl child, that had been found murdered. In his summing up the Coroner, Mr Humphries suggested that as a practical remedy to put a check upon the crime of infanticide, he suggested that they found a hospital where:

'young women would be if necessary taken in until their confinement was over, and then their offspring would be kept and brought up. At the present nothing but absolute ruin threatened mothers of illegitimate children, and to avert it, murder was freely resorted to'.

Once again nothing happened and the menace continued. According to official estimates by 1844 over 3,000 illegitimate children were born and put out to nurse in London every year, and chillingly 'the majority of those die within a very brief period'.

Such a situation became a breeding ground for the baby farmers of Britain who took advantage of women's vulnerability, and her need to keep silent about the child she had given birth to, for those who managed to obtain a situation. By 1866 one of the most dedicated heroes for the suppression of the baby farmers was Mr Ernest Hart, the editor of the *British Medical Journal.* The newspaper ran articles condemning the baby farming system and had found that such places were extensive in large towns and manufacturing districts. The *BMJ* caused a fake advertisement to appear, requesting for a child to be adopted or nursed, and reported that it generated 330 replies. It was found that two thirds of these had 'bad' motives for wanting to adopt. Mr Hart claimed that:

'there was no doubt that many women carried on the system with the deliberate knowledge that the children would die, and with the intention that they should die quickly'.

Another person who condemned the practice of baby farmers was an MP for Salford called Mr William Thomas Charley. The recently formed Infant Life Preservation Society was founded to address the need to tackle the baby farmers. On Wednesday November 9 1870 a group of men led by Mr Charley, waited upon the Secretary of State Mr Henry Bruce at the Home Office. They wanted to enquire into his views with respect to the explosion of baby farming in Britain. Mr Charley requested that 'future legislation be implemented for stopping the practices now carried out, whereby infant life is largely sacrificed'. Mr Bruce listened to the gentlemen at some length before informing them that the Government were inquiring into the subject at that time. The bill for the Protection of Infant Life, which became known as 'Mr Charley's bill' passed its second reading in March 1872. By November the Infant Life Protection Act had come into operation and was now being called the 'Baby Farming Act'. This Act made it illegal for people to obtain money for looking after more then one child, who had not been registered. It also ensured that such premises where these women now practiced their trade were to be regularly inspected, and any found not up to standard were to be quickly closed down. As we have seen the Act failed and neither the baby farmers, nor their premises were registered.

Even when premises were registered it did not stop the deaths. A woman named Armstrong at Plumstead narrowly escaped a prison sentence in January 1878, following the death of a five month old baby called George Curtis. She had been registered for 18 months, and during that time seven illegitimate children had died whilst she was caring for them. Once again the mother was seen to be at fault, and she was highly censored for putting the child in Mrs Armstrong's care. The Act was supposed to gave local authorities the power to have regular inspections of the registered houses, particularly where any deaths of children at the house had been reported. For some undefined reason however it had been decided that the Inspectors would be appointed by the Metropolitan Board of Works. These dealt primarily with the development of the city infrastructure to cope with rapid urban growth. The Government never explained why they had decided that these Inspectors would be responsible to the Board of Trade. Nevertheless they announced that persons wishing to be registered as such 'nurses' may obtain certificates at their office. It had been agreed that the certificates must be signed by a minister of the Established Church, and two respectable rate paying householders. When the certificates were returned, Inspectors would inspect the house to see if the sanitary conditions were fit for the health of a child. By May 1873 it was recognised that the Act was not working, and what's more, if there had been any joy with which the new legislation was received, it was short lived. Accusations were soon made that the law, as it stood at that time, protected the baby farmers rather than condemning them. Another attempt to deal with the problem was also introduced that year. This was the reform of Bastardy Law which had been amended to make fathers equally liable for the maintenance of the child. It also enabled Poor Law Boards to aid mothers in obtaining support for illegitimate children. However this again was difficult to enforce, as men would either deny the paternity, leaving a slur on the woman's honesty, or many would abscond leaving mother and child forced to enter the workhouse.

Baby farming in Victorian Britain only really began to come to an end, due to the efforts of the Society for the Prevention of Cruelty to Children which was set up in 1883 in Liverpool. Other towns and cities quickly adopted its policies, and in 1895 Queen Victoria became its patron and the NSPCC was born and is still in operation today. The Society had been originally formed to prevent children being exploited in the employment market, and at the time no one expected that it would provide a death knell to the baby farmers of Britain. NSPCC Inspectors would take to court, not only baby farmers but also neglectful parents charged with the abuse of their children. A shelter was opened in October of that year, in order to provide a refuge and the Society invited communications of any cases of cruelty to children. These Inspectors found that baby farming was flourishing and many of the cases of child deaths were laid at their door. With the publication of the exploits of Amelia Dyer, who had been in the business for 30 years and was hanged on 10 June 1896 became known, something had to be done. The Infant Life Protection Act of 1897 made it clear that all person having more than one child to care for, must register them with the local Board of Guardians. All deaths should also be registered with the coroner within 24 hours. But how this Act differed from the previous one, was that persons running baby farms must allow inspectors into their property without obstruction. Now local authorities could actively seek out and investigate baby farmers and lying-in houses. Cases were now brought to court from local authority Inspectors, working in conjunction with Inspectors from the NSPCC who had the power to rescue any children found there, and take them to a place of safety

What the development of the baby farming system achieved for society was that it brought to light the need to protect children in the Victorian era. As long as giving birth to a child was regarded by society as a mere peccadillo on the part of a man, and the natural consequence for an immoral woman, ensured that baby farmers would exist and flourish. This kind of thinking protected no one except the baby farmers and held back any effective legislation to abolish this vile crime. But there was still a long way to go as the case of Amelia Sachs and Annie Walters indicates once the Victorian period was over. In 1903, Sachs kept a lying-in house in East Finchley London where she advertised that after the birth the child 'could be left'. Annie Walters would 'adopt' the child and soon after the body would be found, usually poisoned with a mixture of morphine. Once again there was no proof of the numbers of children who had died in this way, apart from the large numbers of children's clothing found at the lying-in house. The two women were executed at Holloway Prison on 3 February 1903. The last baby farmer to be executed in Britain was a woman called Rhoda Willis (aka Leslie James) who was arrested after she returned home drunk in June 1907. Her kind hearted landlady helped her to bed, and was horrified to find the body of a dead child in a bundle by the bed. She was found guilty and executed on Wednesday 14 August 1907.

Only when legislation started to put children's lives first, did an end come to this terrible business. The Children Act of 1908 which became part of the Children's Charter, introduced the registration of foster parent's and finally formed the death knell of baby farming in Britain. Only with the formation of a society that took child protection as it absolute bedrock, was the problem eventually eliminated. Today thankfully, education and loss of ignorance places no judgment on children born to single parents.

SOURCES

NEWSPAPERS USED

Morning Chronicle
Lancet
Derby Mercury
British Medical Journal
Sheffield and Rotherham Independent
Birmingham Daily Post
Liverpool Mercury
Glasgow Herald
Morning Post
Bury and Norwich Post
Huddersfield Chronicle

Standard
Sunday Times
Freeman's Journal
Daily News
Bristol Mercury
Exeter Mercury
Morning Post
Bristol Mercury
Era
Royal Cornwall Gazette

If you have enjoyed reading this book, then here are some more written by the same author and easily accessible to download onto a kindle device immediately or to buy in book form on Amazon. Some are 19th century crimes committed in Britain generally, whilst other focus on the town of Rotherham itself.

Rotherham Crime Books:

MORE NINETEENTH CENTURY ROTHERHAM MURDERS

Many of these cases have been drawn from those published in Margaret Drinkall's weekly column in the *Rotherham Advertiser*, but they have been expanded to include much more details. For example there is a case of a young boys killed by a stagecoach that was travelling too fast along Westgate. There is the murder of a farmer at Thrybergh, that remained unsolved to this very day, despite a reward and an allegation made twenty six years later. There is an attempted murder at the canal side in Rotherham where a man tries to kill his wife. Another man tried to kill his wife at the Dusty Miller public house, by shooting at her. But perhaps the most serious attempted murder was that of a man who tried to kill his former landlord and his wife. He had wanted her to elope with him, but she refused and the actual letters they sent each other are reproduced. In addition there is a case of a shoot out on Wellgate at the Cleaver Inn, and other true crimes such as poaching, highway robbery, infanticide as well as a man who claimed to be imitating Jack the Ripper. All these crime took place in the same lanes and street in which modern people of Rotherham walk along today

ROTHERHAMS ROGUES AND VILLAINS

This book has six new cases, which have never been written about before concerning some of the rogues and villains of the town of Rotherham. The cases include:

An sudden and unprovoked attack on an elderly man, by a younger one he befriended in Conisborough. The two men had formed an unlikely friendship for many years until the sudden, murderous attack which completely came out of the blue. The second case is one which broke a gang of robbers that had been operating in the area around Rawmarsh for many years. The Rotherham police force looked on helplessly as the crimes continued, and which were only broken when four men of the village took the law into their own hands. The third case also holds a mystery. Did a harassed servant girl take her revenge on her controlling mistress by poisoning her, or was she completely innocent pawn? Only you can decide. The fourth case is a massive jewel robbery of which a local rogue, a man called 'King Dick' was strongly suspected. Failure to catch the thieves for this crime, or the many other robberies that remained unsolved in the area, brought the reputation of the Rotherham police force into strong disrepute. The fifth case is a couple who lied and cheated people into supplying them with goods, on the understanding that they would be re-paid. The last case is that of a disaffected solicitors clerk from Wath. When his former employers refused to pay the money that he felt he was owed, he maligned them in placards which were placed in the windows of his house, for all the world to see.

ROTHERHAM CRIMES

This is another book of true crimes in Rotherham which took place in the 19th century. Many of these cases have been published in Margaret Drinkall's weekly column in the *Rotherham Advertiser* but they have been expanded to include more details and the actual statements made by the witnesses and those accused of crimes. The book includes the case called 'Consider Me Dead' about breach of promise case. This expanded version introduces the actual love letters between the couple, plus two vicious ones that the allegedly 'demure Miss Glover' had sent to Mr Straw's ex-girlfriends. There are more swindles uncovered when William and Eliza Fritz came to Rotherham reporting that they had come into money. The tradesmen of the town were eager to supply them with goods and food on the expectation that they would be paid when the couple came into their inheritance. They did not realise they had been duped, until the couple skipped town. There is the mysterious poisoning of a woman called Mrs Bates who was visiting the town from Birmingham. When she died after eating some sausages, the police were not notified and no inquest was held until her husband heard rumours that she had been poisoned. Other case involve a smooth talking clog dancer, the notorious Mrs Barton a brothel house keeper and the strange case of Eli Swift

MISCREANTS AND MURDERERS IN VICTORIAN ROTHERHAM

Who would have thought that on the bridge which still holds an ancient chapel, a man was murdered for no reason at all. By now, most people are aware of the problems facing women giving birth to an illegitimate child in Victorian society. But who would believe that a respectable farmer could impregnate his housekeeper and yet deny all knowledge of it, despite her statement to the contrary. There is a compelling account of an embezzlement at Bentley's Brewery, and the way in which the thief was detected, using common sense police methods, long before the development of the forensic science we have today. The book also has an account of a robbery at an isolated toll bar whose keeper kept a loaded pistol, cocked and ready to fire on the mantelpiece. A neighbours quarrel, which illustrates the low lifestyle of people living in the rabbit warren of yards off Westgate. But the most terrible of all these is the case of the brutal neglect of a father towards his daughter, who in his eyes, brought the ultimate shame to his door.

MYSTERY MURDER AT BOLTON-UPON-DEARNE

On 5 December 1856 two elderly people were murdered in their home, bludgeoned to death during an apparent robbery. The wounds inflicted on them were so severe, that two doctors and the coroner stated that over many years of practice, they had never seen such violence before. Although the case was never solved at the time, new research has brought a possible killer to light. Was he the man who took the lives of these eminently respectable people? With the probable criminal, both victim's families and everyone else safely in their graves, the only person left to judge, is you.

ROCHE ABBEY MURDERS

This is the story of two deaths years apart, which was linked by a man's silver watch. By coincidence, both men were related and both were returning home to the village of Stone near Roche Abbey. Neither made it. In the first case a man was hung for the crime, although many people believed that he was innocent. Twenty three years later his nephew disappeared under strange circumstances, leaving the watch he had inherited, behind.

National Crime Books:

MESSENGERS OF DEATH

It was easy to kill someone in the 19th century, much easier than it is today...

Access to arsenic could be gained for pennies and it's effects mimicked such diseases as cholera, dysentery and typhoid, all of which, at the time, were common illnesses. Other killers, such as laudanum, sulphuric acid and a rare poison called colchicum were used by the women in this book. Research proves that it was easier to kill someone by poison in rural areas than in big towns and cities. In most cases, the murder was only brought to the attention of the authorities by gossip and rumour mongering. One expert suggested that there were many hundreds of poisoning cases that remained undetected. It was said that women were more amenable to poisoning as it was a non physical type of execution. They also had less chance of detection, by travelling around the country, getting married and/or changing their name. The insidious ways in which these poisons were used, called for such women to be nicknamed 'Messengers of Death'.

Using previously unexplored cases, Margaret Drinkall reveals how women poisoners in the nineteenth century created such a culture of poisoning, that it seriously alarmed the government and the legal authorities of the time. Some women believed that spells and the power of witchcraft would protect them from the gallows. One woman offered her services as a professional poisoner, to other wives wishing to escape their husbands.

Many others enjoyed the benefits of murder after insuring their relatives in burial clubs, *without the knowledge or consent* of those who were poisoned. Women in the village of Wix near Harwich used mass poisonings to rid themselves of encumbrances. As a result, local coroners were forced to order many exhumations. This then is the story of some of those 'Messengers Of Death'...

THE OTHER WHITECHAPEL MURDER

This book deals with the true murder of Harriet Lane in 1874. She was the mistress of a middle class business man called Henry Wainwright and she disappeared on 11 September 1874. Exactly a year later to the very day, Henry asked a former employee to help him remove two parcels from his business address at 215 Whitechapel Road. The man Stokes agreed but was curious about the contents and when his former employer went for a cab he peered inside and to his horror found the chopped up remains of a woman. Following the cab Stokes managed to attract the attention of two constables and Henry was arrested with the remains. Shortly afterwards his brother was also arrested and charged with being an accomplice to the murder. This case has all the components of a typical Victorian murder, the body being transported in a cab and the body being covered in chloride of lime which was thought to destroy the remains, but in fact worked as a preservative. Using the newspapers of the period and the reports of inquests, magistrates court enquiries and the trial itself, the tale unfolds revealing many twists and turns. But what caused a frisson in the minds of the newspaper reading public was that Henry had so nearly got away with it. For a whole year the body had remained hidden and if Henry had sent Stokes for a cab instead of getting it himself, he would never have been convicted.

WOMEN ON THE GALLOWS

These are some of the cases of women who died at the end of an executioners rope for varied crimes from infanticide, murder of a grandchild and an uncle, to a woman charged with being a resurrectionist a few years after the exploits of Burke and Hare. Included are an horrific tale of a woman who took children from a workhouse and starved and beat them until some of them died. There is the case of a hard hearted stepmother who murdered her own children and her stepchildren because they were 'in the way'. Catherine Foster was so beautiful that she was called the Belle of Acton, but that didn't stop her from murdering her husband, because she never loved him and didn't want to be married. A young girl hanged for infanticide who tried to appeal to the other women lodging with her for mercy. None was shown to her and she was arrested and sentenced. All these women all ended up being hung and sometimes even these judicial deaths themselves were so horrific, that calls for the end of capital punishment was heard in Britain. Legal brains even discussed alternatives methods of execution which would hopefully be less traumatic.

Printed in Great Britain
by Amazon